COLLECTING

Yellow Ware

BOOK II

An Identification & Value Guide

Lisa S. McAllister

COLLECTOR BOOKS

A Division of Schroeder Publishing Co., Inc.

The current values in this book should be used only as a guide. They are not intended to set prices, which vary from one section of the country to another. Auction prices as well as dealer prices vary greatly and are affected by condition as well as demand. Neither the Author nor the Publisher assumes responsibility for any losses that might be incurred as a result of consulting this guide.

Searching for a Publisher?

We are always looking for knowledgeable people considered to be experts within their fields. If you feel that there is a real need for a book on your collectible subject and have a large comprehensive collection, contact Collector Books.

On the Cover:

Rooster, $1,650.00 and up; Westward Expansion cup and saucer, $195.00 – 245.00; Jeffords Rockingham teapot, $475.00 – 575.00; Bud vase, $150.00 – 225.00; Banded pitcher, $375.00 – 450.00

Cover design: Beth Summers
Book design: Michelle Dowling

Additional copies of this book may be ordered from:

COLLECTOR BOOKS
P.O. Box 3009
Paducah, Kentucky 42002–3009

@ $17.95. Add $2.00 for postage and handling.

Copyright: Lisa McAllister, 1997

Contents

Dedication

To those of you who are interested in yellow ware in the broadest sense... in any size, shape, form, or color...regardless of age or country of origin, I dedicate this book to you. May you have many hours of enjoyment from this book.

Acknowledgments

Photography by:
  Lisa McAllister
  Howard Foster

Items from the collections of:
  Roger and Elaine Cole
  Byron and Sara Dillow
  Howard Foster
  David and Gayle Hitchcock
  Lisa McAllister
  Leslie Miller
  Bernice Woolsey

Thanks to everyone who helped — I couldn't have done it without you!

Firstlook Photo, Hagerstown, MD
Charles and Barbara Adams
Tim Cassady, "Hi, this is Tim, the privy-digger."
D & I Services, for supplies and assistance in developing this book
Glenna Fitzgerald
Gene Haney, for faith in my abilities
Bill Kurau
Bill Lewan
Jonathan Rickard

And to Barry, who did that hausfrau thing...again. If I could clone you, I could retire. Thanks!

Introduction

Yellow ware has achieved much more respect in the last decade. And well it should. Anyone who takes the time to look through the photos in this book will be amazed at the variety of forms. Since yellow ware was produced for over a century we can find anything from an eighteenth century whimsey to a twentieth century utilitarian object. Popularity and demand have brought many pieces to the surface and education has enlightened us to be able to identify previously unidentifiable pieces. Still, yellow ware is not considered to be "serious" pottery by some people.

My purpose in doing this book is to catalog forms of yellow ware not previously illustrated in *Collecting Yellow Ware*. While some of the pieces in this book have been presented in other books on ceramics, quite a few have never been in print before. I also wanted to present new information on potteries and potters' marks. For that reason there is no complete listing of yellow ware potters. The glossary defines terms used in this book.

It is not an easy task to put a value on something that is rarely seen or has never been found before. Therefore, in pricing yellow ware pieces in that category, I have given the low end of the range and up. As far as valuation in general, I have suggested a price range based on what I have seen objects actually sell for. These prices were obtained from different sources — dealers, auctions, antique centers, and collectors.

I personally think that yellow ware is one of the most interesting objects a person could collect. You can actually use it in the kitchen (with care) and in every other room in your home. There are going to be new discoveries, too. If you have curiosity and like a challenge, yellow ware collecting is for you. You will never be bored!

From the computer, at work on book three...

Sincerely,

Lisa S. McAllister

Potters & Their Marks

The following are marked pieces of yellow ware. Since so few pieces are marked many people don't know what the marks should look like. Although some are illegible, if you can identify a shape or cartouche, you can often identify the maker. Instead of presenting you with a long list of potters I recommend that you purchase *Lehner's Encyclopedia of U.S. Marks*. Lois Lehner, the author, illustrates the shape of a mark as well as giving you information on the pottery. This can be very helpful since pottery marks often did not "take" well.

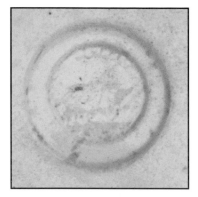

Hound-handled pitcher: Harker, Taylor & Co., East Liverpool, Ohio. 1846 – 1851.

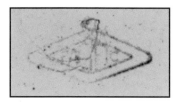

Vase: Pacific; Pacific Clay Products Company, Los Angeles, CA. Approximately 1921 – 1935.

Spittoon: Etruria Works, 1852, East Liverpool; Etruria Pottery, East Liverpool, Ohio. 1844 – c. 1876.

Toby shaving mug: E & W Bennett, Canton St, Baltimore. Approximately 1850 – 1856.

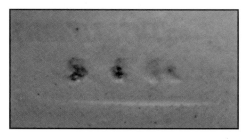

Rabbit mold: Phoenix Pottery, combined with a few indistinguishable letters and numbers; Phoenixville Pottery, Kaolin and Fire Brick Company, Phoenixville, PA. 1867 – c. 1872. This is the first marked rabbit mold that I have ever seen. The design is the typical rabbit mold. This company, after a name change to Griffen, Smith and Hill, began to manufacture majolica. It was molded in shapes of fruit, vegetables, etc. and then colored in bright, multi-colored tin glazes. The interesting thing is that they used yellow ware for the bodies of majolica. This was done c. 1870 – c. 1890.

Candlestick: Jugtown Ware, with an impressed vase; Jugtown Pottery, Seagrove, Moore County, NC. c. 1921 – c. 1960.

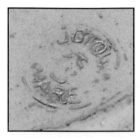

Bowl: The Brighton Pottery Co., Zanesville, Ohio. 1905 – 1907.

Pie plate: T Brunt Derbyshire Warranted Fireproof; Thomas Brunt succeeded his father, John, at their Rawdon Pottery, near Burton-on-Trent in Derbyshire, Great Britain. They started production together c. 1830; Thomas continued in business until c. 1861.

Rockingham-decorated waste bowl: J.B. Patterson Fire-Clay Ware Manufactory, Pottsville, PA; no dates known.

Canning jar: Manley & Cartwright, East Liverpool, Ohio. 1864 – 1927.

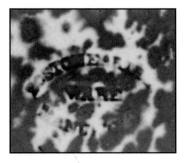

Baking dish: Boston Earthenware Manufactory; c. 1850s.

Teapot: American Pottery Co., Jersey City. 1833 – 1857.

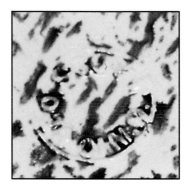

Spittoon: G. Scott Cin. O.; George Scott, Cincinnati, Ohio. 1853-54 – c. 1900.

Mold: Bourne; Joseph Bourne & Son Ltd., Bourne's Pottery, Denby, Derbyshire, Great Britain. Approximately 1809 – 1860.

Mold: I.W. Cory Trenton, NJ; Ira W. Cory Pottery, Trenton, NJ. Approximately 1867 – 1870.

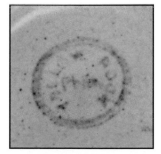

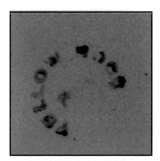

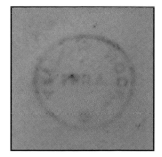

These utilitarian pieces, a miniature mold, a baking dish, and a butter crock, are all marked by the Yellow Rock Company in Philadelphia. These marks and the ones made by the Jeffords Pottery are the most common marks on yellow ware. No dates have yet been discovered for the operation of the Yellow Rock Pottery. They did use some of the same molds as the Jeffords Pottery. That means that they were either in business at the same time as Jeffords or perhaps bought Jeffords' molds after they went out of business. Yellow Rock may have been the trade name for the Philadelphia City Pottery Company, who advertised themselves as the successors to Jeffords. They made similar wares. Some of Yellow Rock's mini-molds are copies of tin molds made in England in the early part of this century. That may be one clue to their dates of operation.

This banded mixing bowl and Rockingham-decorated saucepan bear two of the four known marks from the J.E. Jeffords Pottery. The other two marks are: an impressed mark identical to the diamond-shaped ink stamp, and an uncommonly seen 3" long elliptical mark (usually found on oval baking dishes). The mark on the Rockingham piece is uncommon. The patent date is June 28, 1870; the dates of operation for the company are 1868 – 1915. They started in business as the Port Richmond Pottery Company.

Canning jar: Robert Arthur's Patent 2nd January. 1855. Arthur Burnham & Gilroy. Philadelphia. This company marketed these jars as fruit jars. 1854 to at least 1860.

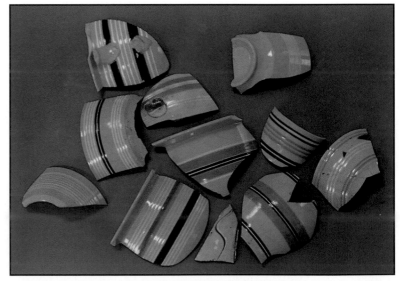

Pottery shards are one way to make discoveries about what potteries produced and where they were located. Old privies or outhouses are excellent sources for shards since they were used as dumps. The homeowner would have used ceramics that were locally made as well as imported. The shards above were dug from an early privy in Baltimore, MD. The privy had not been used after 1850. There was a preponderance of yellow ware shards that had the same clay consistency and color. They were all decorated in colors of blue, brown, and white slip. The slip was applied as bands or as earthworm (see the earthworm-decorated batter bowl and the catseye mug). There was obviously a pottery in that area producing these pieces. The forms found are utilitarian mugs, pitchers, waste bowls, and chamber pots.

A word about Canadian yellow ware. There are many pieces of utilitarian yellow ware that have been attributed to American and English manufacture but were actually made in Canada. Canada was quite active in yellow ware production, mostly because they had to compete with American factories for business. In the 1870s American firms were going full steam ahead in yellow ware production (although much of it was covered with Rockingham). The Brantford pottery in Canada started to produce similar pieces and because of their variety of production became the largest manufacturer of this type of goods in the country. They produced the following: slip banded bowls in the style of waste bowls (rimless and with a foot), molded pitchers, usually with Rockingham decoration, molded yellow ware bowls, pie plates and nappies (plain and with Rockingham), molded spittoons, molded teapots, funnels, and even picture frames. There are yellow ware molds attributed to them, too. They also produced seaweed mocha decorated bowls. The seaweed is blue and sparse on a wide, white slip band; under the white band are two slim brown slip bands. The placement of the mocha-decorated band is directly under the rolled rim. They sometimes covered their yellow ware with green (funnels) and/or blue sponge-type decoration. The bulk of this pottery was produced from about 1873 – 1883. Brantford was not the only Canadian firm producing yellow ware (among others were Cap Rouge Pottery and Tara Pottery) but they were definitely the leader.

Westward Expansion

In this chapter I wanted to illustrate as many different forms of this type of pottery as I could find. It is known as Westward Expansion or Westward Ho because of the motifs embossed around the rim. They are: Indians, covered wagons, cavalry flags, buffalo, campfires, and cowboys.

There has, as of yet, been no definitive answer as to where this pottery was made. England cannot be ruled out because of the vast amount of china they made for the American market. Ohio seems very likely, especially in light of the types of transfers sometimes found on this pottery (see the chapter on Plates, Platters & the Like). An enormous quantity of transferware with similar designs was made in Ohio at the time that I think these pieces were produced about 1925.

The clay is thin but heavy. The clay color is a deep yellow, with a tendency to be pumpkin-colored in the center. Pieces for the table seem to have been the only forms made.

I have heard of the existence of a covered vegetable dish but was not able to obtain a photo for this book.

Soup plate, 9". $165.00 – 195.00.

Cup and saucer, $195.00 – 245.00 each. Cups, $100.00 – 125.00. Saucers, $50.00 – 65.00.

Gravy boat. $295.00 – 375.00.

Fruit bowl, 6". $125.00 – 150.00.

Open vegetable bowl. $295.00 – 375.00.

Plates. 6", $100.00 – 125.00. 9", $165.00 – 195.00. 11", $175.00 – 250.00.

Covered sugar bowl. $325.00 – 375.00.

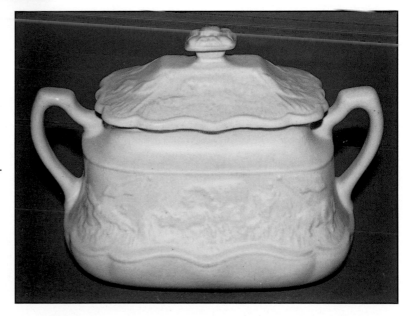

This is a rare washboard. The scrubbing area is composed of four separate "plates" of yellow ware, two of which are covered with a dark brown slip. All of the square plates are attached to the wooden frame with copper nails, which are inserted through a hole in the center of each plate. Standard size, 1880 – 1910. American. $575.00 and up.

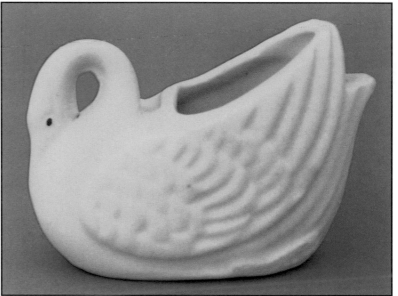

Swan-shaped toothpick holders were made in blue and white stoneware, as well as yellow ware. The clay is buff-colored with stone in the body. Midwestern, c. 1910. 4" long. $100.00 – 150.00.

Jugtown Pottery in North Carolina made a variety of simple, utilitarian things. Their yellow ware is not the typical yellow clay that you see in most yellow ware and their pieces tend to be less refined. This candlestick dates from the 1920s to the 1960s. 7¼" diameter. $125.00 – 195.00.

Rare wall plaque with embossed bust of George Washington, covered with white slip. Really a wonderful piece! The back is unglazed; the front has heavy crazing. Primitive looking due to its lack of detail. Probably English. Early nineteenth century. About 4"x6". $850.00 and up.

Miniature flower pots are quite rare. I think it is remarkable that this one still has its saucer. The silver lustre trim is not too worn. This is English, made about 1830. Only 2⅛" tall. $250.00 – 350.00.

It is hard to find a miniature bowl and pitcher set like this with only white bands. The bowl is a bit more shallow than usual. England, 1870 – 1900. Only 3" tall. $800.00 – 950.00.

Wedgwood made this set of two candle snuffers and tray. They are rare when found in yellow ware. The length of the tray is 6⅝", the snuffers are each 2¼" tall. About 1840. $450.00 and up.

Most yellow ware cradles have incised and Rockingham decoration. These examples are plain yellow ware with basketweave embossing. They were originally made as christening gifts. 3¾" to 4½" long. England, 1810 – 1830. $525.00 – 625.00 each.

Yellow ware rolling pins with advertising are rare. Oddly enough, the ads usually refer to undertaking! The replaced handles on this pin do not decrease the value. American, 1890 – 1920. $500.00 and up

This is a match safe, the ribbed area being for striking the match. An unusual form in yellow ware, it has light blue slip bands top and bottom. Note the low glaze, making it more effective for its intended purpose. 2½" tall. American, circa 1900. $175.00 – 225.00.

These were known as spice shakers and were made by the Morton Pottery Co. in Morton, Illinois. They are normally found with green and brown sponged decoration, called Woodland so they are rare in plain yellow ware. They were part of the "Amish Pottery" line introduced in 1929. There is obviously yellow in the glaze and a now-worn-off red and blue transfer on the front. Each, $200.00 – 295.00.

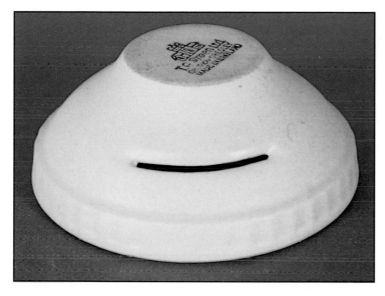

This is an egg separator. You can clearly see the mark on the bottom — T.G. Green, Ltd.(England). This church mark was first registered in 1888, but the date of manufacture on this piece is early twentieth century. 4" in diameter. $65.00 – 95.00.

This is a reed pipe, so-called because the stem would be a piece of grass or other similar plant life. These pipes are frequently found in stoneware, rarely in yellow ware. It was dug from a privy in Baltimore, MD. Nineteenth century. $75.00 – 125.00.

The blue sponging on this footwarmer has dripped so as to give it the look of an optical illusion. This triangular form is not common. Footwarmers took a lot of abuse — don't expect to find them in perfect condition. Amazingly, this one *is* perfect. The length is 11¼" and it was made in Ohio. Nineteenth century. $500.00 and up.

This rare piece is a bedwarmer. It would have been placed in the coals to absorb heat and then put into the bed to warm those cold nights without central heating. Due to the nature of its use (or abuse) not many would have survived, even in poor condition. 19th century, American. 8"x6"x1¼". $300.00 – 400.00.

Purely decorative, this late eighteenth century shoe is a real rarity. The Rockingham sponging on the exterior mocks the Whieldon glazes of the same era. 7" long. England. $600.00 – 700.00.

Most of the match safes made in this form were covered by a colored glaze, so it is very hard to find one that is plain yellow ware. This example is 6⅜" tall and was made during the 1930s, probably in Ohio. $495.00 – 625.00.

Before the advent of window screens you needed this pair of lions — they are window rests. Notice how the potter made a hollow area behind the lion's mane to facilitate picking it up. The Bennington pottery made some window rests, too — they are total opposites of these. Theirs were thick and chunky; these are hollow and made of thin clay. The faces are very folksy. I like the fact that they are plain yellow ware. I'm sure you already know they're rare. England, about 1810 to 1820. 4" tall. $850.00 – 950.00 for the pair.

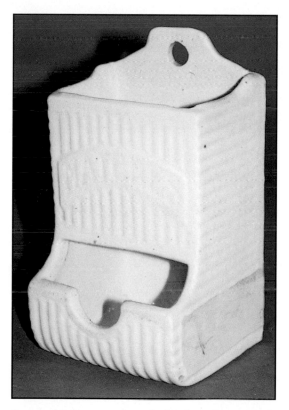

Brush-McCoy marketed this hanging match safe as part of its "KOLOR-KRAFT" line. Luckily, at least one escaped the brightly colored glazes that they used. This was made during the 1930s. Although you could strike your match anywhere on the ribbed surface, there is an unglazed area on the side at the base, just for that purpose. 6¼" high. $525.00 – 625.00.

The Bell Pottery in Waynesboro, PA, made a limited amount of things in yellow clay. Many of them were decorated with this brown glaze. The most common piece they did in yellow clay is a canning jar; this jug is one of the most rare. You may be able to see the stamp near the neck. The height is 13". $2,000.00 and up.

These are miniature flower pots. The tallest is 3". The embossed decoration outlined in gilt identifies them as being late Victorian England or European. $100.00 – 150.00 each.

The brown bands are indicative of pieces made by Weller in Ohio. This is a child's feeding dish. Its wide, shallow form and heavy clay, for stability, made it perfect for the job. 1930s. 7" in diameter. Infrequent in yellow ware. $150.00 – 195.00.

Two unusual forms made during the 1920s and 1930s. A bucket with a twisted handle, only 3" tall, and a paneled bud vase, 7" tall. Midwestern. $150.00 – 225.00 each.

This is a case where a potter substituted yellow ware for his usual clay, white earthenware, or pearl ware. The decoration was incised by hand, not molded. What a great find for a yellow ware collector. 8" long. Made in England about 1815. $1,000.00 and up.

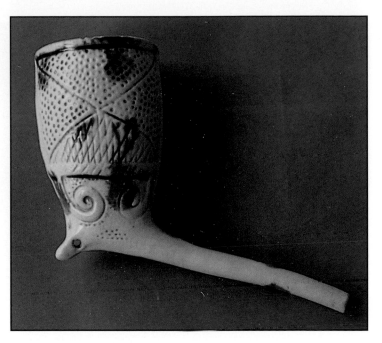

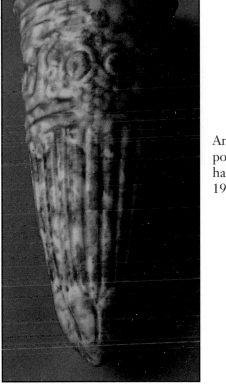

An experiment in yellow ware, wall pockets like these are normally seen in art pottery. This one was made by Brush-McCoy in Ohio. The style of the Rockingham is the same as on their Nurock line of yellow ware. 8" long and made about 1915. $135.00 – 185.00.

Canadians produced yellow ware like this sponged funnel. Even though they are later than the plain yellow and Rockingham examples they still have merit and are scarce. Actually, the form is referred to as a jar filler but the two terms seem to be interchangeable (except to purists!). $325.00 – 400.00.

You will rarely see slip cups like this for sale. Many are in museums, since few people have private, study collections of pottery. I think it is interesting that yellow ware was so widely used that it was even made for tools. This slip cup is further elevated by having a name and date. Maybe the "C & C." stood for C.C. Thompson & Co. of East Liverpool, Ohio. 10" long. $750.00 and up.

This model of a Gothic chapel has incredible detail. Every single brick is represented, along with the doors, windows, and even the clock face! These pieces are normally found in pearl ware with polychrome decoration. I'm glad a potter tried one out in yellow ware. 10" tall. England, c. 1820. $1,500.00 and up.

Miniature pitcher and bowl sets have become increasingly scarce. These mocha-decorated examples are exceptional. It is well worth purchasing these pieces separately; the bowls are much harder to find than the pitchers. Left, $1,650.00 – 1,850.00. Right, $1,350.00 – 1,550.00.

Bennington made urns in yellow ware with colored glazes but I don't know if they made this one. I like the tiny patches of brown and blue. This urn consists of the flower pot and the stand. The bottom of the flower pot is unglazed and fits into the top of the stand. 10" tall. $350.00 – 425.00.

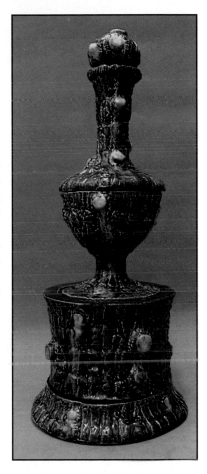

After this I guess you've seen everything! This is a smoking stand. It was made in England, third quarter nineteenth century. The Rockingham glaze and the molded design imitate a tree trunk. It breaks down into 5 pieces: the plate (for eating), on the bottom; the humidor (tobacco); the goblet; the candlestick; and the candle snuffer, at the top. All made for the man of the house after a hard day. Height is 17½". $600.00 – 700.00.

This rare piece is a vinaigrette. They held smelling salts and the like, and were carried by ladies in case of a fainting spell. This is the only one that I have ever seen in yellow ware. It has a pewter top and is 3" long. Either English or European, nineteenth century. $400.00 and up.

It is unusual to see yellow ware with historical motifs. The Centennial of the United States would have been celebrated during the period of time that this teapot was made. Perhaps it was made in tribute to that event. Height 8". $550.00 – 650.00.

As an experiment, a potter dipped this Jeffords teapot in brown glaze. The glaze settled into the recesses of the molding and really brought out the detail. 8" tall. $475.00 – 575.00.

This tall coffee pot is attributed to Otto Lewis when he worked in Mechanicville, NY. The Rockingham decoration on his pieces has a distinctive look. The clay is typically light yellow. A magnificent piece of yellow ware and very hard to find. Mid-nineteenth century. $1,000.00 and up.

On the left is a basketweave molded teapot originally used as a giveaway with Windsor Baking Powder. 5" tall. Made in Ohio. Right, a smaller teapot molded with a design of blackberries and basketweave. This could have been made in England. By now you've probably noticed that the woven design was used a lot on teapots. Left, $450.00 – 550.00. Right, $395.00 – 495.00.

Teapots molded with the design of "Rebekah At The Well" are ubiquitous. They were made from Maryland north to Vermont and even in Canada. Although it is harder to see the embossed design on the teapot shown, this coloration is more desirable than the usual dipped version. The size also makes it an atypical Rebekah because it is 10½" tall (holds 16 cups!). Late 1800s. $350.00 – 450.00.

Banded teapots are few and far between. This one has incised bands filled with light blue slip and rouletted decoration near the rim and on the lid. England, pre-1850. 8" in length. $1,500.00 and up.

This is a teapot with many interesting features. The molded tabs hold a wire bail handle with a wooden grip. Instead of pottery tabs to hold the lid in place, the wire from the handle extends inward. It has a tricolored glaze that indicates it that may have been made in Ohio. The letter "S" is impressed on the bottom. Late nineteenth century, 5" tall. $475.00 – 550.00.

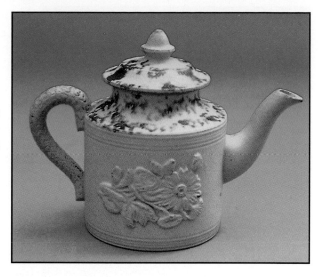

This one-cup teapot has a lot of detail for such a small piece. The applied floral decoration has great detail and is rarely seen on yellow ware. The molded handle and Rockingham-type decoration give it extra appeal. England, made about 1815. $600.00 – 700.00.

The teapot on the left has embossed florals and ribbing and is only 2¾" tall. On the right is a tall teapot (or short coffee pot) with engine-turned decoration. The handle and spout appear outsized for the delicate body. The height is 8". Both are English, c. 1840. (While the clay is a pale yellow, it is darker than in the photograph.) Left, $395.00 – 500.00. Right, $675.00 – 795.00.

Since I have seen sugar bowls and cream pitchers with this same decoration and form I know that this teapot was part of a child's tea service. England, 1830 – 1840. 7" in overall length. $395.00 – 495.00.

A band of agate mocha decorates this 6½" tall chocolate pot. The slip colors in the band complement the deep yellow clay. There is also a raised, beaded design filled in with white slip. Rare! England, 1800 – 1820. $1,500.00 and up.

From the modern shape of this little pot I date it in the first quarter of this century. Only 4" tall and uncommon. Probably Ohio. $225.00 – 295.00.

Scottish potters produced wonderful yellow ware, like this tea set. It is marked Cumnock (the name of the pottery) NB (for New Brunswick) on the teapot. The sugar bowl and waste bowl carry typical Scottish advice. The white slip has a sgraffito (or scratched) design which was polychromed. The sugar bowl is missing the lid — there should be a matching cream pitcher. About 1860 to 1870. $1,000.00 and up for the set.

A pie plate with exceptional pink lustre decoration. 8½" in dia. Mid to late nineteenth century. $225.00 – 275.00.

There is a Colonial Revival type polychrome transfer on this pair of Westward Expansion soup plates. The predominant colors are lavender and black! A thin silver lustre band separates the rim from the serving area. (For more data on Westward Expansion see pages 9 – 11). $150.00 – 175.00 each.

Hard-to-find pie plate in Woodland (green and brown) colors. From the Morton Pottery in Morton, Illinois. About 1930. $175.00 – 225.00.

Rare, nested set of platters or shallow serving dishes. American Pottery Co. in New Jersey also made this form but their pieces are distinctive because of their pale yellow clay. These are English and are about 40 years later than those made in New Jersey. 9" to 11" in length. Set, $1,050.00 – 1,200.00. Each, $300.00 – 375.00.

Wedgwood made this plate with a delicate pink lustre design between 1924 and 1930. It's impressed "Made in England," a mark which all ceramics were bound by law to carry after 1891. $175.00 – 250.00.

The openwork design on the rim of these plates is called arcading. The arcading is enhanced with silver lustre. It would be difficult enough to find one of these plates but here we have seven! 7" in diameter. England, 1820 – 1830. $125.00 – 175.00 each.

This is the second of two different transfers seen on Westward Expansion pieces. The transfer is floral, in green, orange, and lavender on the 9" salad or luncheon plate. Somehow I can't imagine that the pieces with transfers were very popular. $150.00 – 175.00.

These 9" plates have a brown transfer of flowers and a bird with polychrome decoration. They were made by Wedgwood (England) and were part of a breakfast set (Honeybuff) produced around 1939. $75.00 – 100.00 each.

A deep dish, resembling a soup plate, but meant for baking and serving. 9" diameter. 1850 – 1880. $175.00 – 250.00.

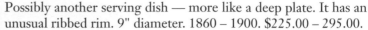

Possibly another serving dish — more like a deep plate. It has an unusual ribbed rim. 9" diameter. 1860 – 1900. $225.00 – 295.00.

This bread tray is a rare form in yellow ware. They are normally seen in white ironstone. The harvest motif (wheat) was a common theme of decoration. Embossed around the rim is "GIVE US THIS DAY OUR DAILY BREAD." The green and brown colors create added interest; they were obviously applied in a pattern. Note the golden yellow clay color. American, 1850 – 1900. $450.00 – 550.00.

These colors (green and brown), when applied in this manner and on creamware, are referred to as Whieldon. The time period is the late eighteenth century. This, however, is a yellow ware plate with a shell or feather edge molded border. This is a great, and rare, piece of yellow ware. England. 8½" in diameter. $500.00 and up.

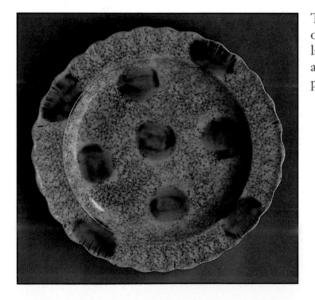

Embossed shells and coral rim this unusually shaped yellow ware tray. This piece may have been made for a tea service. Note the gilt around the rim — this dates it c. 1870. England or Europe. $225.00 – 275.00.

This 14" bowl has a rare design of squiggly slip. You can feel a sense of motion in the slip bands. Mid to late nineteenth century, New York or New Jersey. $1,000.00 and up.

A great, rare piece, this earthworm batter bowl was made in Baltimore, Maryland, in the 19th century. The slip bands at the top are indicative of pieces made in this area. The looped earthworm is well defined. Worth buying in any condition. 11" diameter. $2,000.00 and up.

Notice how the looped earthworm on this waste bowl has a three-dimensional look. It would have taken a very skilled decorator to achieve this. Possibly American, 19th century. 6½" in diameter. $1,000.00 and up.

An unusual form, this cereal bowl dates to around 1920. Probably Ohio. $65.00 – 95.00.

A thick bowl with shallow detail, this example is marked "Yellow Rock, PHILA." When found, these bowls are in the smaller sizes, about 5" to 6" in diameter. $75.00 – 125.00.

This low, ribbed bowl is actually a rice nappy. Only a few have ever been found in plain yellow. (Also found with a Rockingham sponging.) This one is 7" in diameter. Pennsylvania west to Ohio, nineteenth century. $225.00 – 325.00.

Fabulous slip decoration on this large bowl. Don't pass it up because of damage! 1850 to 1880, American. 14" in diameter. $350.00 – 400.00.

It is rare to see a Rockingham decorated waste bowl. This piece is marked by the Patterson Pottery in Pottsville, PA. (See section on marks.) The pottery also produced molds decorated in the same fashion. 6" in diameter. $375.00 – 475.00.

Probably an experiment at the Brush-McCoy factory, this set of five bowls has a wide blue slip band under the typical three white slip rings. 5" to 10" diameter. Made about 1920. $350.00 – 450.00 for the set.

A great banded design on this marked Jeffords bowl. 12" diameter. $275.00 – 375.00. The pottery also produced colanders with the same decoration (although there wouldn't be much room under the slip bands for the holes!).

Hand-painted, overglaze flowers in brick, white, and green decorate this yellow ware basin. The clay is a deep orangy-yellow. 8" in diameter. 1850 – 1880. $150.00 – 225.00.

A low, basin-shaped bowl with a "beaded" rim. I have seen this form with both American and English marks. It has stoneware mixed in with the yellow ware body. See the gray spots on the rim? They are stains from use, and because of the stone in the body would not disappear if the piece were professionally cleaned. 1860 – 1900. $150.00 – 225.00.

The bicolored, floral seaweed is spectacular on this batter bowl. It is heavy and well done. Mocha-decorated batter bowls of this quality are almost impossible to find. This one is English, probably made between 1840 and 1880. 11½" in diameter. $2,000.00 and up.

Brush-McCoy made this bowl as part of their decorated "Dandy-Line." In this line (with bluebirds) they also produced: a bread jar, a pitcher, a hanging salt crock, and a nested set of three round-sided covered butter jars. They were only in production for a short period, obviously, since they are so difficult to find. They may have only produced one size of the bowl. From 1915 to about 1925. $195.00 – 250.00.

I did not mention dates when describing these molds — they are nineteenth century, generally. I have noted the exceptions.

Clarity of design is very important on the common molds. On the rare or unusual examples, however, it is not as important. For example, if you held out for a deep, clear impression in the elephant mold you would most likely never own one. The same rule is true for condition. If you stop to think about how molds were used you will understand why some of them look the way they do! (Turn one upside down, hold it by the base and shake it as if you were un-molding food.) There were many more corn molds made than elephant molds, so we have to accept some damage and lack of clarity on the more scarce pieces. Restoration is also acceptable but it is a subjective thing.

The most common designs in molds are: elongated octagonal wheat, corn, and grapes, and the average size swirl mold (about 4½" diameter). Turkshead molds used to be common. Some of the more unusual ones in this chapter are: the Rockingham swirled muffin pan, the elephant, and the asparagus, to name a few.

The molds shown in this chapter were made all over the world: Canada, Holland, France, England, and of course, the United States.

Elephant. Rockingham exterior, possibly made by Patterson in Pottsville, PA. Has been found in pearl ware. 7⅝" long. $500.00 and up.

Asparagus. 7" long. $450.00 – 550.00.

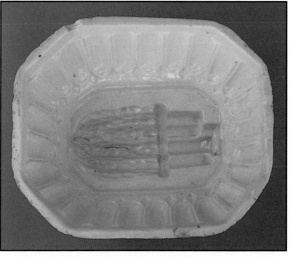

Miniature turkshead. 3½" diameter. Bennington, VT. $150.00 – 225.00.

Swirled muffin pan. Wow! Rockingham on both sides. Measures 14⅞"x10¼". $1,250.00 and up.

Grapes. Sharp detail. 4½" long. $150.00 – 175.00.

Single tree leaf. 4" diameter. $250.00 – 325.00.

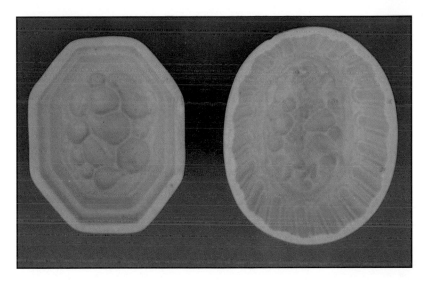

Fruit and vegetable clusters. 6" to 7" in length. $250.00 – 350.00 each.

Stars. 4½" to 5" diameter. $350.00 – 450.00.

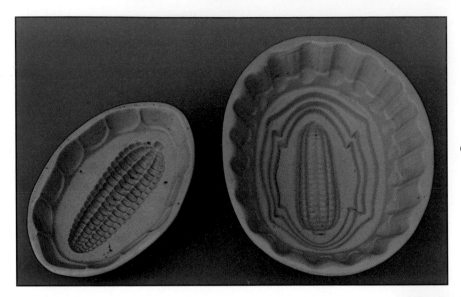

Corn. 7" to 8" long. $125.00 – 165.00.

Pineapple (large). 8" long. Has been found in pearl ware. $375.00 – 450.00.

Fish. 7½" long. $350.00 – 450.00.

Turkshead with exterior scalloped rim. 9" diameter. $175.00 – 250.00.

Loaf mold with advertising. "A.W. GROSE Manufacturer." $395.00 – 495.00.

Geometric. Note the heavy glaze pooled in the bottom of the mold. After 1900. 7" long. $225.00 – 275.00.

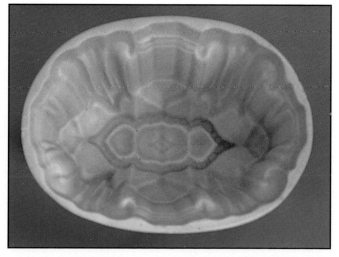

Corn. 9½" long, one of the largest in yellow ware. $135.00 – 175.00.

Grapes. Tiny cluster in a deep mold. 5½"x6½". $165.00 – 225.00.

A cluster with fruit, wheat, and a walnut. Possibly after 1900. Two holes in the foot rim for hanging. 9¾" long — another big mold. $250.00 – 350.00.

Large flower — a dahlia? Shaped like a basin, with an extended rim. 7¾" diameter. $350.00 – 450.00.

Modern-looking flower. I have seen this design block printed on wallpaper. The first time that I've seen one of these molds marked, the larger (7½") one is marked "I.W. CORY" (Trenton, NJ). $275.00 – 395.00.

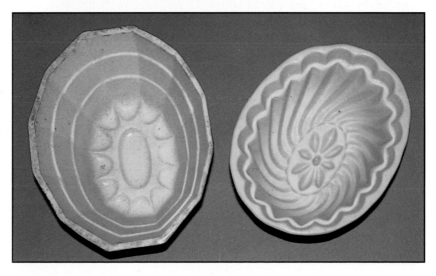

Geometric. Left, Rockingham exterior. Stepped on outside also. 7½"x6". Right, marked Sharpes (England). 7"x5½". $200.00 – 250.00 each.

Miniature molds. These are 13 of the 15 (at last count) different ones that I have found. Generally 3" in diameter. Whether they are marked (Yellow Rock, Phila.) or not doesn't really affect the price. $125.00 to 250.00 each, depending on the design.

A delicate cluster of flowers. 7¾" long.
$300.00 – 375.00.

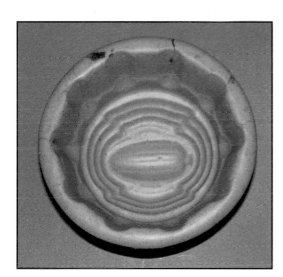

Corn. 4" diameter. $140.00 – 175.00.

Sheet mold with berries. This was a candy mold.
9⅛"x7⅛"x1½" thick. $175.00 – 250.00.

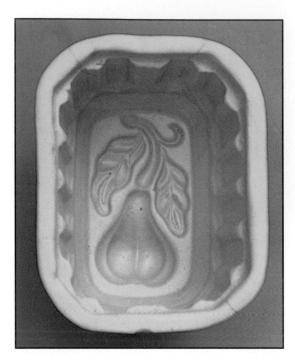

Pear. A deep mold. 4"x5". $325.00 – 425.00.

A hen with her chicks. 4½" long. Has been found in pearl ware. Marked "BOURNE" (1840s). $450.00 – 550.00.

Rabbit. This one is different — it shows the rabbit in profile, sitting in front of a bush. 6"x4¾". $450.00 – 550.00.

A different swirl, marked "JOHN BELL" (Waynesboro, PA). Rockingham exterior. 4½" diameter. $625.00 – 695.00.

I think that this is an artichoke. Deep. 6¾"x4½". $395.00 – 495.00.

These are the two remaining mini-molds of the 15 designs that I have seen. They are also the most rare. The smooth heart is almost impossible to find; until 1995 I had not seen the swirl design in the mini-mold size. The swirl has the semi-circular blue ink stamp instead of the circular black stamp. (At least they were consistent — if you find a swirl mold marked by Yellow Rock it will always have the semi-circular blue stamp.) $200.00 – 250.00 each.

This Rockingham-decorated shoe is a double inkwell. 4" long. Nineteenth century, possibly Ohio. $225.00 – 275.00.

Plain, primitive cone-shaped inkwell, 2½" tall. This shape is similar to many glass inkwells. Yellow ware inkwells like this one are not often found. Nineteenth century, American. $175.00 – 225.00.

A rare piece, this inkwell with a reclining doe was produced in East Liverpool, Ohio. The deep base held quite a lot of ink and was probably not meant for home use. The heavy brown and green glaze totally obscures the yellow clay color but fortunately not the detail. Nineteenth century. 8" long and about 7" tall. $1,800.00 – 2,200.00.

Lift the lid from this grape cluster to find a double inkwell. Overall length is almost 8". The gilt trim and subject matter define it as being English or European. 1860 – 1890. $250.00 – 350.00.

It is rare to see a toy chamber pot with sponged decoration. The blue color on the yellow ware gives it a greenish cast. Late nineteenth century, probably Ohio. $200.00 – 250.00.

Another toy potty of the typical size but with rare decoration. The black transfer, "FOR A YOUNG SPORTS-MAN" is the type of thing usually seen on early English children's china. Pre-1850. $500.00 and up.

Two unusual potties. Left, "ALL GOING OUT AND NOTHING COMING IN" in brown slip (how apropos!); "BK 500" also in brown slip on the bottom. The other potty has no decoration whatsoever. Both were produced at the Morton Pottery in Illinois. They date from 1900 to 1925. Left, $150.00 – 200.00. Right, $200.00 – 250.00.

Although a usable size at 5½" in diameter, I think this potty was made as a gift. At the top in white slip, "GO WAY BACK AND SIT DOWN" (a popular verse on toy potties), at the bottom "BILL RECEIVING SET MARY." The white slip bands in the middle are the same design used by Brush-McCoy in Ohio around 1915.
$350.00 – 425.00.

A variety of toy potties, banded and mocha decorated. The average size of a toy potty is 2" tall and 2½" in diameter. 1880 to 1920. Banded, $125.00 – 165.00 each. Mocha decorated, $195.00 – 295.00 each.

This toy potty is not only larger than usual (but still not of practical size), but it has green seaweed decoration — rare on toy potties. It is English and c. 1900. Measurements are 3" tall and 4⅝" in diameter. $350.00 – 425.00.

I think that this was a soap dish. It has a faintly molded design of a bird on a branch. The clay is thick and pale. Probably American, c. 1900. 5" long. $250.00 – 325.00.

These banded pitcher and bowl sets are harder to find. Many times you will find the pitcher without the bowl. The black and white bands are indicative of T.G. Green Pottery, Church Gresley, England. 1890 to 1925. The pitcher would be 8½" tall. The set, $650.00 – 800.00.

This diamond-shaped spittoon is a rare form among spittoons. The outside has a better-than-usual molded design of hounds. The Rockingham glaze is applied nicely, allowing much of the yellow clay to show through. 11" long. Possibly Ohio, nineteenth century. $200.00 – 300.00.

Interest in collecting yellow ware colanders has brought many to the surface. Even though there are more around they are still considered scarce, and even rare. Expect hairlines and cracks, especially between the holes. Chipped foot rims are common, too. I'm sure many were dropped! Also, the holes in the pottery stress the stability of the piece as a whole.

A great blue and white banded colander, marked by Jeffords, Philadelphia. The more bands a colander has the more valuable it can be. The diamond-shaped clusters of holes near the bottom are decorative, but not too practical, on a colander this large. c. 1870. 14" diameter. $1,200.00 and up.

This brown and blue banded colander is a rarity among banded colanders. It also has an interesting clay — almost orange in color. Note the dark blue specks on the light blue slip band. Possibly Pennsylvania, 1860 – 1890. 8" diameter. $1,200.00 and up.

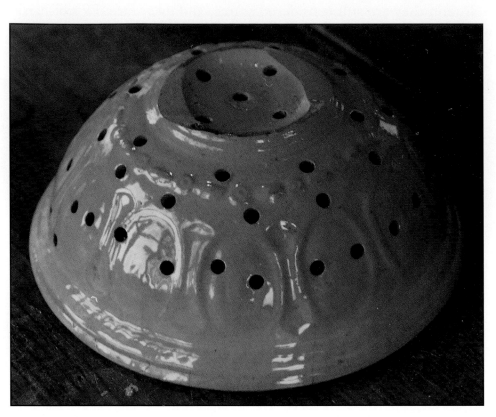

Although this is an easily found colander I show it here to illustrate the large, widely spaced holes, and the foot rim made to facilitate tipping the bowl to either side. Early twentieth century, England. $100.00 – 150.00.

Plain yellow ware colanders, like the one on the left, are assumed to be American but can sometimes be English, like the embossed example on the right. 1880 – 1920. Left, $395.00 – 525.00. Right, $100.00 – 150.00.

Another great banded colander marked by the Jeffords Pottery. (You can see the mark, faintly, on the bottom of the piece.) Many of the banded colanders seen were made by Jeffords and the Yellow Rock company. Brown and white banded colanders are harder to find than blue and white examples. 13" diameter. $1,200.00 and up.

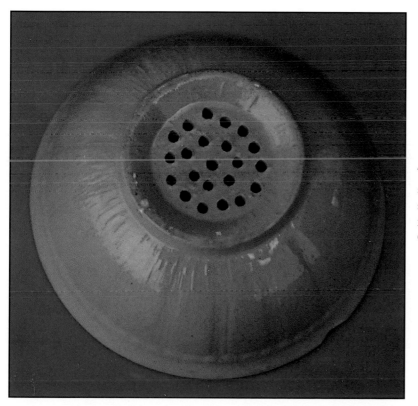

This is a funny little colander. It was probably an experiment — there are very few drain holes and no holes for hanging. There is also embossing but it didn't come out of the mold too well. Ohio, c. 1900. 8" diameter. $350.00 – 450.00.

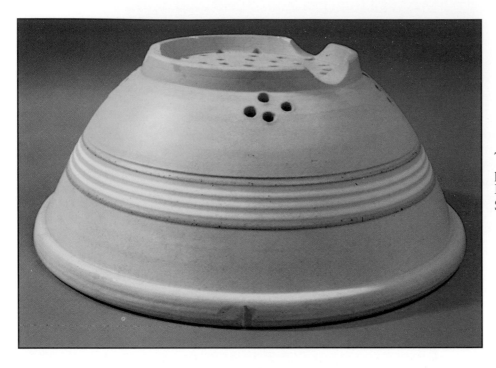

Typical blue and white bands for a piece marked "YELLOW ROCK PHILA." C. 1870. 10" diameter. $1,200.00 and up.

The multitude of slip bands on this colander don't show up too well because the clay is so light. The holes seem like an afterthought and are not very practical. Like most colanders the holes are punched in a pattern. 10⅜" diameter. American, 1860 to 1890. $800.00 – 900.00.

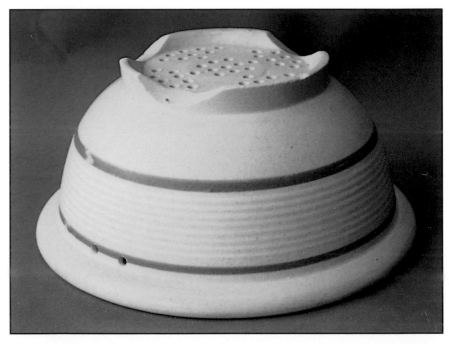

Not only is this one of the most rare decorations possible on a yellow ware colander, but the colors are rare, too. Earthworm is typically some combination of blue and/or brown and white. This earthworm is light blue and white with some green. Those colors are echoed in the slip bands. Not that it matters much, but on the negative side there isn't a lot of contrast. See the incised lines? They were drawn to give the potter an idea of placement of the holes. 12" diameter. Pennsylvania or New York, c. 1860. $4,000.00 and up.

I think this piece speaks for itself. The strong brown and white earthworm and slip bands make for great contrast. The yellow ware mocha collector's dream. Most likely New York State. 1850 – 1870. 10¾" diameter. $5,000.00 and up.

Green oxide decoration on an egg cup with a thin body. All egg cups are rare at this time, and not very many are American. Nineteenth century. $325.00 – 395.00.

The egg cup on the left has thick clay and a primitive look. It is attributed to Otto Lewis, Mechanicville, NY. The form is different from the typical egg cup. Mid-1800s. On the right is a cup with heavy pink lustre decoration from Spain. Both are 2⅞" tall. Left, $395.00 – 495.00. Right, $200.00 – 275.00.

Brown and white banded egg cup, England, c. 1900. $395.00 – 495.00.

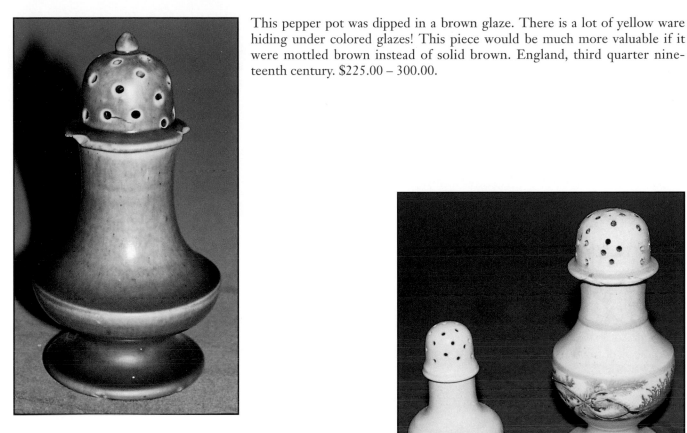

This pepper pot was dipped in a brown glaze. There is a lot of yellow ware hiding under colored glazes! This piece would be much more valuable if it were mottled brown instead of solid brown. England, third quarter nineteenth century. $225.00 – 300.00.

The pepper pot on the left is only 3" tall and was made by Wedgwood in England, c. 1900. The pepper on the right is rare because the blue seaweed is in a floral pattern. Generally, small pieces of yellow ware mocha do not display any pattern in the seaweed. England, 1860 – 1890. Left, $250.00 – 350.00. Right, $650.00 – 750.00.

This is just a small sampling of the shape and decoration found on yellow ware pepper pots. The average height is 4¼". All are English, 1850 – 1900. Blue seaweed, $550.00 – 650.00. Red seaweed, $1,000.00 and up. Banded, each, $475.00 – 595.00.

Although this piece is banded like others in the Zane Grey line (Hull Pottery), it was not a production or molded piece. It is hand turned with an applied, flat pedestal base. The base is incised "G.M.," the initials of the potter. Kind of a homemade master salt. The clay is thick; the height is just a few inches. $250.00 – 325.00.

These two disparate and rare pieces coexist nicely. The tricolored earthworm on this master salt is like beads strung on a necklace. It dates from 1840 to 1860. The pepper pot has a combination of embossed slip and sanded decoration. It dates 1860 to 1890. Both are English. Master salt, $1,000.00 and up. Pepper pot, $550.00 – 675.00.

This group of seaweed mocha-decorated master salts shows a range of shape and color. The rounded-bowl master salt with blue seaweed is the most common yellow ware master salt found. The straight-sided bowls are less common. English, 1850 – 1900. Rounded blue seaweed, $375.00 – 495.00. All others, $495.00 – 650.00.

A nice group of banded master salts, the one in the center being the most common. Master salts are generally 2½" tall. English, 1860 – 1910. Each, $350.00 – 525.00.

Even though their production period was short because they were easily broken, we seem to find an endless array of canning jar shapes and sizes. You can count on damage at the rim — absolutely perfect jars are a rarity! (They were probably never used.) Lids, which could be pottery, metal, or wax, were applied and removed many times, hence the sometimes gross amount of damage at the rim. Most jars are missing their original lids. Very few are not American. These jars date from around 1840 to almost 1900.

The slip-banded jar on the left is rare, while the one on the right is fairly common. The blue-banded jar was made in Baltimore, MD. The jar on the right was manufactured by Church Gresley in England, c. 1900, and was described as a "Brown Top Jar." Left, $225.00 – 275.00. Right, $85.00 – 125.00.

This very sturdy-looking jar has a wax sealer rim. The rim is ridged, so it would work like teeth to bite into the wax and hold it. A wax sealer is a disc of wax that is about 3½" across and about ¼" thick. 7" tall. $175.00 – 225.00.

From left to right: an Illinois wax sealer with holes for a bail handle, 8" tall; a Maryland jar with an inner rim to support a lid, possibly a cork, 5" tall; another Midwestern jar with lots of stone in the body and a sharp raised design. Also a wax sealer made to accommodate a bail handle. Note the difference in clay consistency between the three jars. Left, $150.00 – 195.00. Middle, $125.00 – 165.00. Right, $225.00 – 275.00.

The three jars in this photo are from Ohio and Illinois. Left and middle are wax sealers. The barrel one is unusual in that is not — most barrel canning jars *are* wax sealers. It is also without the vertical, incised lines done to imitate wooden staves. 6" tall. Left, $150.00 – 225.00. Middle, $150.00 – 225.00. Right, $125.00 – 175.00.

A Midwestern wax sealer with an infrequently seen embossed design. 6½" tall. $175.00 – 235.00.

The narrow form of this cylindrical jar makes it appear taller than its 6½". $150.00 – 200.00.

A wax sealer with a softly scalloped rim, made to accept a bail handle. 7¼" tall. $150.00 – 185.00.

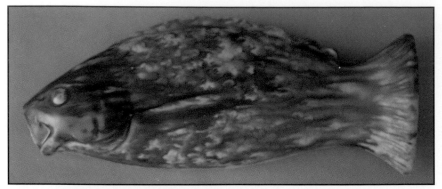

Fish flasks can be found in Rockingham or plain yellow ware. The body and scales are molded but the tail design was incised by hand. 9" long. England, third quarter nineteenth century. $850.00 and up.

I am partial to this bottle because it has so many interesting features. Bulkley Fiske & Co. was a retailer whose vessels, like this one, were made in Trenton, NJ. The body has concave panels and a great handle — a folksy, smiling snake. The sponged glaze is cinnamon-brown and teal blue. 10¾" tall. Mid to late nineteenth century. $800.00 and up.

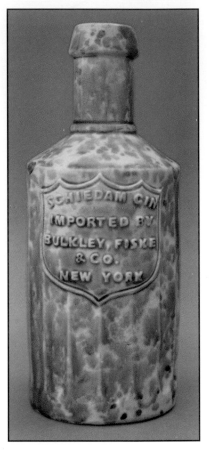

This 3" tall piece appears to be a small cruet. It has a tiny pouring spout and an odd handle, almost too small. The Rockingham decoration is nicely variegated. Ohio, 1880 – 1910. $225.00 – 275.00.

Bulkley Fiske used these man-shaped bottles to deliver their product. This one has great detail — the fluted sleeves, the buttonholes, and that face with the crooked smile. 10" tall. Nineteenth century. $800.00 and up.

I have to make a note about the next three bottles. Before 1995 the only pig bottles I had seen were the molded ones that are identical to some pig banks (see the Ohio Rockingham pig bank on page 72). Then I purchased these three. They are the only ones I had seen in over 10 years of looking for yellow ware. At least two of the three were made in Anna, Illinois, at the Kirkpatrick Pottery. Among other things, the Kirkpatricks were known for making pig bottles incised with maps of railroads and covered with brown slip. The form of two of these three bottles is identical to Anna pigs, and there is an example of the Kirkpatricks using Rockingham as a glaze. The bottles were initially cylinders and then finished by hand. The detail is shown to its best on the plain yellow bottle, not only because it has the best detail but also because colored glazes tend to overshadow details. (True in a lot of examples.) All of the pigs are anatomically correct. The use of the pig as a form for the selling of liquor is no accident. Hogs and corn are staples of the agrarian Midwest. The date of manufacture is roughly 1870 to 1890. I was excited about these pieces and hope you will find them interesting, too. For more details about Anna pig bottles check the bibliography for the book on the Kirkpatrick pottery.

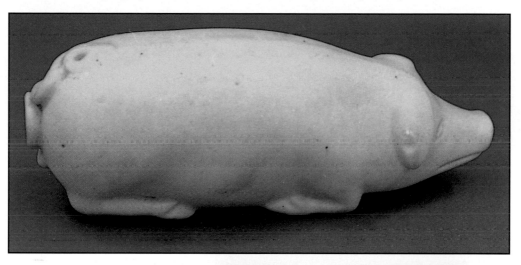

7½" long. $1,800.00 and up.

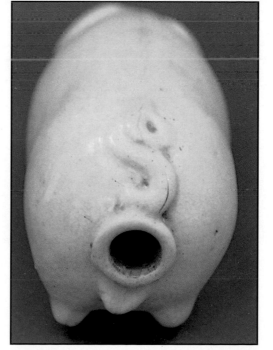

This pig has the mouth of the bottle in his snout. Generally, the mouth of the bottle is at the opposite end of the pig. 6½" long. $1,500.00 and up.

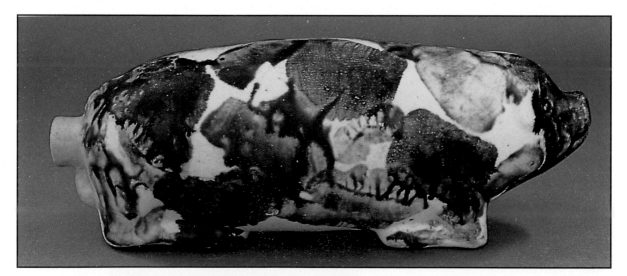

I am not sure about this pig having been made at Anna, but it does look similar. I have seen an identical form in redware marked by the Shenfelder pottery in Reading, PA. 8½" long. $1,800.00 and up.

Yellow ware banks are still hard to find although more have surfaced recently. Generally, the pig banks (the most common form) are American, while the other forms seen are English. Dates of manufacture vary widely, covering nearly an entire century. Most banks have some type of sponged glaze, usually Rockingham, which can be found alone or combined with other colors. There is a wide variety, but animals are the most frequently seen.

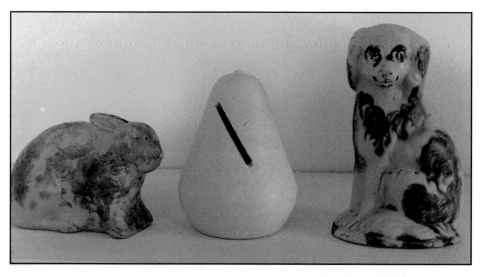

Rabbit, nineteenth century, England. 3½" in length. $375.00 – 450.00. Pear, c. 1900, Austria. $175.00 – 250.00. Dog, nineteenth century, England. 4½" in height. $350.00 – 450.00.

Church, nineteenth century. 3½" in length. $250.00 – 350.00.

 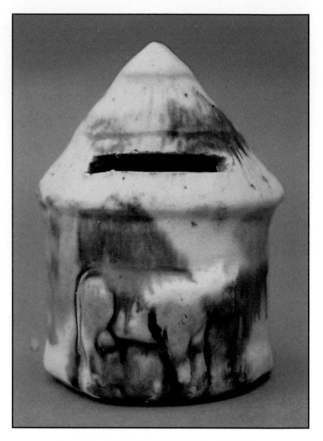

One of my favorites — a cottage with a cow. Nineteenth century, English. 3½" tall. $375.00 – 450.00.

The "finial" above the coin slot is actually a miniature jug with a handle. Nineteenth century. 7" tall. $350.00 – 450.00.

English spaniel, c. 1840. Height 4½". $350.00 – 450.00.

Early English. 3¾" long. $350.00 – 450.00.

These pigs are usually white earthenware with a yellow glaze. Early twentieth century. 4" long. $175.00 – 225.00.

American, c. 1900. 5" long. $200.00 - 250.00.

Nineteenth century. 2" tall. $150.00 – 200.00.

Both banks are Scottish, nineteenth century. Left, 3½" tall. $165.00 – 225.00. Right, 7" tall. $275.00 – 375.00.

Chick, c. 1900. 3" tall. $200.00 – 250.00. Bear, c. 1900. 5" tall. $250.00 – 350.00.

House, nineteenth century, England. 3¼" in length. $325.00 – 425.00. Cat, also nineteenth century. 4¼" tall. $350.00 – 450.00.

Thick clay. Coin slot on back. Nineteenth century, England. 7" long. $350.00 – 450.00.

A typical Ohio pig bank, sometimes seen in plain yellow ware. Rarely, they were made as bottles with a hole in the back end of the pig. Note the mold line running horizontally the 5" length of the body. C. 1920. $100.00 – 175.00.

The top half of this hive-shaped bank was dipped in brown glaze. 5½" tall. American, c. 1900. $165.00 – 225.00.

An appealing blue and white band combination on this posset cup. This one is about the size of an average coffee cup. English, c. 1860. $375.00   425.00.

Primitive, embossed shaving mug. Thick clay with a thin glaze. Nineteenth century, American. $250.00 – 325.00.

Wedgwood made these mug and saucer combinations. They are demitasse-sized (the equivalent of a single order of espresso). It's great to find six at one time! English, of course, and c. 1900. Each, $125.00 – 150.00. As a set, $900.00 – 950.00.

Strong black seaweed design on a large mug. Very good clay color with narrow white rings. Yellow ware decorated with black seaweed is harder to find than almost any other color. Height is 5". Probably English, third quarter nineteenth century. $950.00 – 1,050.00.

Embossed tankards like this one are normally found dipped in a green or brown glaze. The fact that this one "escaped" makes the value much greater than a dipped example. Morton Pottery, Morton, Illinois, c. 1925. 5" tall. $125.00 – 175.00.

This is a beaker or tumbler. It was made at the Bennington Pottery in Vermont, 1844 – 1858. The height is 3½". $275.00 – 325.00.

This posset cup with a name and hand-painted floral decoration is one of the best pieces of yellow ware I have ever seen. It is from England, c. 1830. Height is 2¾". $550.00 – 625.00.

Posset cups are often mistaken for toy chamber pots. A flat rim identifies it as the latter. This posset cup has an earthworm/marbleized decoration. The foliated handle has an interesting treatment and is a clue that this piece was made in England. c. 1840. 2½" tall. $550.00 – 650.00.

The mug in this photo has a decoration similar to rouletting. It has a nice form and an interesting American handle. Yellow ware mugs with no color whatsoever are difficult to find. Height is 3½". $225.00 – 295.00.

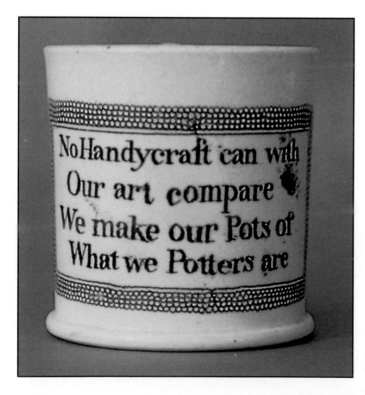

Verse transfers like the one on this child's mug are usually seen on pearl ware. It's rare to see one on yellow ware. The verse is a popular one. England, c. 1830. $450.00 – 550.00.

The banding on this large mug is indicative of decoration done by the T.G. Green/Church Gresley Pottery. England, c. 1900. $125.00 – 175.00.

This green seaweed mug is devoid of any detail except surface decoration. It's earlier than most mocha-decorated mugs. Height is 2¾". England. $350.00 – 400.00.

Rockingham goblets such as these were made at Bennington, Vermont, and probably other potteries as well. They exhibit that white lining which was thought to make pottery more sanitary. Not easy to find, they date c. 1850. 5½" tall. Without handle, $300.00 – 350.00 each. With handle, $375.00 – 475.00 each.

This oversize mug with frogs and a lizard was made as a joke for a pub or tavern. The very decorative handle was made for support when the mug was full. An interesting feature is the half of a frog inside the bottom — to make the drinker think he had swallowed the missing part. One of the great pieces of yellow ware. England, c. 1850. $1,000.00 and up.

This odd looking pieces is a stirrup cup. They are almost unheard of in yellow ware. It is decorated with enamel colors on a thin clay body. Damage on a rarity like this is quite acceptable (but this example was mint!). English and very early, about 1815. 5¼" long. $1,000.00 and up.

Yellow ware tumblers are quite rare. This one has a lot of seaweed for a small piece, in a blue branching design. The turning at the foot is a nice touch. 4" tall. England, c. 1840. $950.00 and up.

Stirrup cups were used during a fox hunt. The rider could slip it into his pocket and pull it out for a drink when he stopped at houses along the way. This Rockingham example is English and dates to about 1830. 4½" long. $1,000.00 and up.

This American mug has exceptionally wide bands which make up for the sparse amount of blue seaweed. 4½" tall. Possibly Ohio, c. 1890. $400.00 – 495.00.

A rare mug! This mocha pattern consists of tiny, oval depressions filled with very dark brown slip outlined in white, known as engine turning. It is a design not often seen. The pink lustre creates added interest and rarity. 4" tall. England, c. 1830. $1,000.00 and up.

The mug on the left shows an unskilled but interesting mocha pattern, loosely described as earthworm or cable. It is average height but a bit more narrow than usual. The mug on the right is more plain in design but rare because the decorator touched the white areas of the earthworm with green oxides. Mugs like these two are very difficult to find. Both are about 3" tall; c. 1850. Left, the English mug, $750.00 – 850.00. Right, American, $750.00 – 850.00.

The simple mocha on this mug was done by an unskilled worker. There is no obvious design, just slashes of bicolored slip. The slip bands are not the usual ones seen on a mocha-decorated piece like this. American, c. 1850. Height is 3¼". $550.00 – 650.00.

A grape motif is embossed around the rim of this mug and then accented with Rockingham. This combination of embossing, clay color, and application of Rockingham is indicative of English manufacture. Height is 2¾". C. 1890. $165.00 – 225.00.

Completely plain yellow ware mugs are very hard to find. The mug on the left is a typical form, while the mug on the right is not. It appears more modern. Both are first quarter twentieth century, American. Left, 3" tall. $125.00 – 175.00. Right, 4½" tall. $150.00 – 225.00.

This mug is rare because it has a spout. It probably had a lid. The blue and white bands give it a soft appearance and are in an unusual pattern. Most likely English, 1870 to 1900. $300.00 – 375.00.

Either a presentation or a giveaway for the Cincinnati Cooperage Company. Two small children are getting drinks from a cask, with grapes embossed on the other side. The glaze looks like those used at the Morton Pottery so it could have been made there. Height is 7". Probably made around 1930. Not common. $400.00 – 500.00.

This white-lined mug has a molded seal applied on the slip band, opposite the handle. It was either a presentation piece or to represent a trade union. Notice the handle: this mug, when full, would be quite heavy, so the potter made the handle of a size and shape to accommodate. The user, however, needed more leverage, so he cut a piece out of the rim at the handle. There is more control of the mug when the tip of your thumb is resting in the groove (I know — I tried it!) Last but not least, the floral seaweed design is one of the best. One of the best pieces of mocha existing. English or Scottish, third quarter nineteenth century. $1,000.00 and up.

At 3" in diameter and only 2" tall, this mug may have been made for a special purpose. The blue and white band combination is not average either. Probably English, 1870 – 1910. $300.00 – 400.00.

The brown and white swirled slip design on this mug falls into the mocha category. Notice how the design at the base of the mug matches the design on the handle, with pleasing results. 1840 – 1880. $650.00 – 795.00.

I think that this mug, with its tricolored cat's eyes, was made in Baltimore, MD. The clay color and consistency, and the style of decoration, fit with other pieces made in that area. About 1850 – 1880, possibly earlier. $795.00 – 895.00.

I like the feeling of motion caused by the wavy slip bands on these mugs. Both are a bit larger than usual (average mugs measure 3½" x 3½"). Mugs with decoration like this are rare. American, 1850 – 1875. $650.00 – 750.00 each.

On the left is a tankard with early green seaweed in a great scenic tree design. Note the white lining. England or Scotland, 1840 – 1870. On the right, a slightly concave body with very sparse Rockingham decoration. Probably not American. 1850 – 1880. Both are rare. Left, $1,000.00 and up. Right, $450.00 – 550.00.

Yellow ware tankards used to be uncommon; now they are rarely seen. Should you find one it will most likely be a banded example like the ones at right. Tankards are defined as being taller, at least 5", than they are wide, giving them a slim rather than chunky appearance. These examples are 5" to 6" high. They were made in America and Great Britain. 1860 – 1900. $550.00 – 695.00 each.

Figures of animals have always been popular. They were made in every type of ceramic available, yellow ware being one of the rarest. Their production seems to be limited to the nineteenth century. Most have some type of Rockingham decoration, whether a few small spots or entirely covered. A few figures are found with blue sponging — examples are spaniel doorstops or the lion inkwells made at East Liverpool. Sizes range from a few inches to one foot in height. Some of the most primitive looking pieces are the earliest made. None of them are common. Expect damage on the base, especially on the larger ones. All of the figures in this chapter were made for decorative purposes, although some of the larger ones doubled for doorstops. For more (utilitarian) animal figures check other chapters.

Primitive, folksy lion figure about 3" long. Hollow. England, c. 1830. $375.00 – 450.00.

This dog is more stylized than most other spaniels. Notice the separate foreleg, unusual and a mark of quality. The thin, hollow body is 9" tall. Probably English, c. 1860. $550.00 – 650.00.

It is hard to believe that someone would create an attractive pieces like this to be used as a doorstop. The body is thick and heavy. It was molded and then the face and mane were detailed by hand. Mr. Lion has a permanently surprised look. The hollow base is dated 1868. 8" long. American. $750.00 and up.

Small figures such as these were considered toys. They are English and were made in the mid-1800s. The dog measures 4" long and 3½" tall. Each, $350.00 – 450.00.

Bennington made spill holders in the form of deer, like this one, and also cows. (Sometimes they were made without the spill just for mantel ornaments.) They could be Rockingham decorated or flint enamel. The odd looking clumps are called coleslaw — except that they are pottery, not edible. Deer in mantle ornaments like this one were molded with holes in the head and the horns were added later...or not. Length of 10¾" and dating 1844 to 1858. $8,500.00 – 10,000.00.

Bennington made this pair of plain yellow lions. At the museum in Vermont there is an inkwell with Rockingham that is identical to these lions. They may have been an experiment. Since most of the yellow ware made in Bennington had some type of colored glaze, anything that is plain yellow is scarce. 4¾" in length and dating 1853 – 1858. $750.00 – 850.00 for the pair.

This pair of Scottish spaniels is outside the usual range of yellow ware collecting, because that yellow clay is nowhere in sight. The hollow bodies were dipped in white glaze and then decorated in blue, green, and brown. The heads and baskets are picked out in more colors for added detail. The molded baskets are a rare detail on yellow ware dogs. This pair of dogs is one of my favorites. Height is 7½". They date c. 1860. $1,500.00 and up for the pair.

Two more toy figures — a dog and a woman. Both are hollow. The dog resembles a pug and is short on spots. It is 3¼" tall. The woman has tiny sponged spots in atypical colors of russet and Wedgwood blue and is 5" tall. Both are English and date c. 1840. Each, $450.00 – 550.00.

This small figure of a rabbit (also called a hare) was made in Yorkshire, England. The price of a piece such as this has more to do with subject matter and the manufacturer than the fact that it is yellow ware at all. It has very broad appeal, not just to collectors of yellow ware. A rarity. Made about 1810. 4" tall. $1,500.00 and up.

The decorator of this pair of spaniels had a sense of humor — these guys have mustaches and Groucho Marx eyebrows. The octagonal bases are a nice feature. 7" tall. New Jersey, c. 1870. Each, $475.00 – 550.00. Pair, $1,200.00 – 1,400.00.

Cats are not seen nearly as often as dogs in pottery. They couldn't have been as popular as they are now! These are attributed to Ohio, nineteenth century. Although both are yellow ware, the cat with the least amount of Rockingham is the most desirable. They may have been made to be used as doorstops. Both are solid and quite heavy. Height is 12". Mostly Rockingham, $1,200.00 and up. Mostly yellow ware, $2,000.00 and up.

Toy lamb figure dipped in Rockingham. 2¼" long. England, c. 1860. $250.00 – 350.00.

These dogs were dipped in a thin glaze of Bristol slip, then decorated in blue and brown. Pairs of animals are usually not decorated identically, so don't be concerned if they don't match. One dog is always a little taller than the other, about ½". 7½" tall. Possibly Canadian, nineteenth century. Pair, $1,400.00 – 1,650.00.

Hollow English lamb with brown and white slip decoration. The decorator on this piece looks like he was in a hurry, just daubing on some color and off to the next one. C. 1830. 3⅝" long. $450.00 – 550.00.

It's hard to imagine how magnificent this is unless you've seen it in person. The detail is exquisite, the color a rich yellow. The hollow base is 11" long, while the height is 12½". What a doorstop! American, c. 1870. $2,000.00 and up.

Cobalt sponging on spaniel doorstops is rare. This is a better-than-usual example because of the separate foreleg and the well-done base. Ohio, c. 1880. Height is 10", length, 7¾". $875.00 – 995.00.

Lion mantel ornaments are not common in yellow ware. This pair is only 5½" in length on hollow bases. The lions themselves were dipped in Rockingham glaze, with the bases left plain yellow ware, a nice contrast. The bases appear more primitive than the lions, which were molded. South Amboy, New Jersey, c. 1870. Pair, $1,250.00 and up.

To find an early cow group like this in yellow ware is remarkable. The Yorkshire potteries in England were known for this particular color combination of mulberry and black. The quaint calf and the spotted decoration give this piece a primitive look. About 1810. 6½" long. $1,650.00 and up.

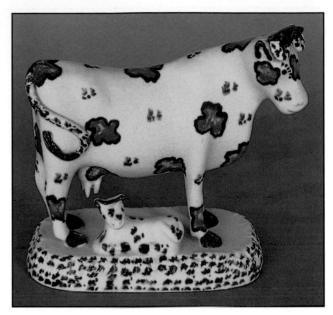

This cow group looks very primitive due to its lack of detail. There is a spaniel instead of a calf on the base and the farmer has struck a pose. It has a combination of molded and hand-modeled details. 6½" long. England, 1810 – 1820. $1,850.00 – 2,000.00.

These great yellow ware birds are very early, made around 1810 to 1820. They have exquisite detail — every feather and even the ears incised by hand. The quail has bivalve shells molded between the feet. They have a wonderful, primitive quality. A little over 7" tall each. English. Rooster and quail, $1,650.00 and up, each.

The black seaweed design is strong on the deep orange band on this mustard pot. The slim white rings set off the whole. England, 1860 – 1890. $550.00 – 650.00.

A watery green oxide decoration was daubed around the neck and on the finial of this sugar bowl. The clay is thin and a pale yellow. Possibly European, nineteenth century. 4¼" tall. $350.00 – 450.00.

This is a rare form for a yellow ware sugar bowl. The black floral seaweed is very well done, and the blue slip rings accentuate it nicely. The lid has a tiny hole in the top for aeration. This piece would still be well worth buying even if the lid were missing (although at a lower price). Ohio or England, 1850 – 1880. $1,600.00 – 1,800.00.

This figural mustard pot is one of my favorite pieces. It combines a rare piece with something that has a sense of humor. It's along the lines of the toby pitcher. Height is 4". English, 1850 to 1880. $475.00 – 595.00.

Two rare mustard pots, with or without lids. Left, tiny dots of seaweed are placed to form an outline of flower, stem, and leaves. Notice that the design on the lid is not floral, yet this is the correct lid. On the right is a polychrome decoration that looks Pennsylvania Dutch (actually a contraction of Deutsch, for German). Both are average size. Possibly American, 1860 1900. Left, $650.00 – 795.00. Right, $350.00 – 450.00.

Simple, white-banded mustard pot with lid. There is quite a variety of slip-banded decorations found on mustard pots but one with just white bands is one of the least common. Possibly American, 1850 – 1900. $350.00 – 450.00.

The type of decoration seen on this sugar bowl, incised and filled in with blue, can be found on many different forms — pepper pots, pitchers, mugs, etc. Notice again that the lid and base do not match identically in decoration, yet this is the correct lid for this base. There is a fine line at times in determining whether or not a lid and base should go together. Only experience will help you in this. England, 1850 – 1900. $450.00 – 550.00.

It is uncommon to see a yellow ware sugar bowl with this much slip decoration. It's 4¼" tall which seems to be the standard size. All sugar bowls, because of their scarcity, still have merit without their lids, although at a much-reduced price. Possibly American, 1850 – 1880. $550.00 – 675.00.

Red seaweed is the most difficult color to find (of course, it's usually the most money). Notice that the seaweed on the lid is not as intense as on the base. This was not as important then as it is today, when people are used to having everything just right. Also, many potteries were relatively small and couldn't affort to throw out something that didn't match. The base has straight sides, seen less often than the rounded sides. England, c. 1870. $1,000.00 and up.

This sugar bowl is very different. It is not only embossed (with berries of some sort), but also has a mottled glaze that is blue, brown, and green. Sugar bowls that are part of a tea service (and this one was) are usually bigger than the teapot. 7" tall. Ohio, c. 1900. $350.00 – 450.00.

From the clay color and the style and color of the Rockingham, this mustard pot looks as if it were made at Bennington. In any case, it's rare to find a Rockingham-decorated mustard pot. The lid is flint enamel. 2¾" tall. Third quarter nineteenth century. $400.00 – 450.00.

The earthworm design on the base of this sugar bowl is very simple while the lid is decorated more elaborately. The earthworm is well defined, having a three-dimensional look to it. The pair of white slip bands give it a softer appearance. Rare! England, 1840 – 1870. $1,000.00 and up.

This shape is referred to as Boote's 1851 Octagon when found in white ironstone. Occasionally, potters substituted yellow ware in their molds, probably as an experiment. This may be why this dish exists, and why so few are found. Nineteenth century. 12½"x8½". $300.00 – 350.00.

This is a butter dish. It was copied in yellow ware from ones made in earthenware as early as 1780. The molded design on the lid and cover really adds to the overall look. See the tiny, dark dots that look as if they were sprinkled over the entire piece? These are air bubbles caused by overfiring in the kiln. Expect damage on the cow finial should you ever be lucky enough to find one of these pieces. England, c. 1860. 7" in diameter. $850.00 and up.

Although this appears to be a tureen, without the pottery cover it is not. It had a metal cover with a central hinge and one lid that opened up from each end. I have had two similar pieces in white ironstone and they were called ice cream servers. I saw a server like this one years ago but, foolishly, did not buy it because the metal lid had deteriorated. That one was marked Yellow Rock. Pennsylvania, c. 1870. $800.00 and up.

Strong navy blue, ribbed bands on this hard-to-find keeler. For some unknown reason many keelers have blue, or a combination including blue, for slip bands. Mid to late nineteenth century. 7½" in diameter at the top. $300.00 – 400.00.

I am not sure what this was made to store. It's very small — measuring 1⅞"x3⅝". The body has fired "hard" and glossy. Note the concave band at the top of the base to facilitate picking it up. And what luck to still have the lid! American, mid to late 1800s. $275.00 – 325.00.

English storage/butter crock with "sanded" band. These pieces date to the late 1800s. Most sanded pieces made for kitchen use have a white lining. About 5" in diameter. $175.00 – 275.00.

Whenever you see this particular band combination in these colors you can be assured that the piece was made by the Yellow Rock Pottery in Philadelphia. These storage crocks are difficult to find; Yellow Rock probably did not make very many. C. 1870. $175.00 – 275.00.

This is part of a set of kitchenware made by the Hull Pottery. The embossed wheat design is also on the lid. There are big canisters like this one, Flour; some others are Coffee, Tea, and Sugar. Also made were small canisters — Pepper, Allspice, Ginger, etc. You might find a hanging salt if you were lucky. Note: These canisters were also made in white pottery with a yellow glaze. Don't be fooled. Large canisters, $225.00 – 275.00. Small canisters, $175.00 – 250.00. Hanging salt, $250.00 – 350.00.

Someone added overglaze painting to this humidor after it was fired (there are also green tulips on the lid). About 5½" tall, it is English or European and dates to the third quarter of the nineteenth century. $175.00 – 225.00.

A lot of the yellow ware that comes from Scotland is decorated in these colors. These canisters can be found printed with contents other than the ones shown. As you can see the application of sponging will vary. 10" tall. Nineteenth century. $275.00 – 350.00, with lid.

Great clay color adds to the overall appeal of this storage crock. It has a lot of embossing but isn't overpowering. The finial on the lid is easy to grip, which is probably why the lid is still around! I think that this crock dates to the third quarter of the nineteenth century, but I have not decided positively if it is English or American. $550.00 – 650.00.

What an impressive piece of yellow ware, and mocha decorated to boot! This form is seen rarely in pearl ware; in yellow ware it is, to date, unique. The fist-sized blue seaweed flowers look as if they are strung on a chain of matching blue seaweed. The fine blue lines give it a finished appearance and add just the right touch. 12" in diameter. Nineteenth century and probably English. $4,000.00 and up.

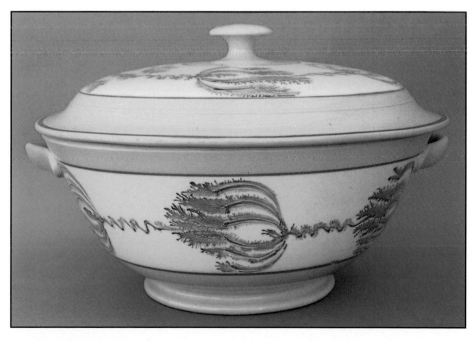

When you see this covered custard cup you wonder how many custard cups originally came with lids. This type of lid would be difficult to hold on to, especially when wet. Not many of these pieces are found still together. American, 1900–1930. $75.00 – 110.00.

This is another mystery — what was it meant to store? The brass-hinged lid has a very small cutout and just slips down over the sides of the canister. Early twentieth century, American. 8" tall. $125.00 – 175.00.

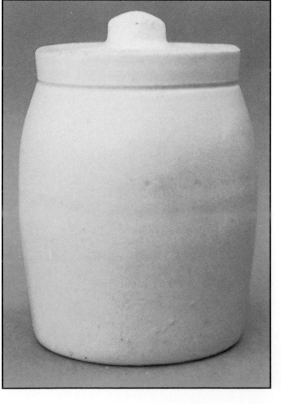

These thick jars are often found unglazed on the outside and painted with flowers. (Don't try to get all of the paint off — it just doesn't happen!) They really are bordering on being 100% stoneware, which can appear yellow and has fooled many a person. This cookie jar is 9" tall. Twentieth century, Ohio. $95.00 – 125.00.

During the Napoleonic Wars flour was in short supply. Persons who were used to being served a dish like this one, entirely made from dough, could forget it! Some smart potter invented the game pie dish, where the pie was now baked in a pottery liner and served in this dish. These were made in many different types of pottery but yellow ware seems to be the least common. You will see many more of these dishes unglazed on the exterior (referred to as cane ware) than glazed. The glazed examples are more popular (and more money) at this time. England, pre-1840. 12" long. $1,200.00 and up.

This is the most common design on a keeler. These have been found in four different sizes so far, all 5" in diameter or less. Although the white lining is no guarantee of English origin I think that these are English. $295.00 – 395.00, each.

A *big* butter crock, measuring 7"x 8". Yellow ware with white bands, no other colors, is harder to find. For some reason there just wasn't as much of it made. See the flaked areas? This can be caused by too little water in the clay mixture before firing. Nineteenth century, American. $175.00 – 250.00.

Beater jars have become more and more popular with yellow ware collectors. They certainly are practical for a variety of things, not the least of which is their original purpose. Oddly enough, most are not found with the beaters, although that is a problem easily solved. Left, Ohio, c. 1920. Right, also American c. 1920, rare in plain yellow. Each, $145.00 – 185.00.

Very few of this form of storage jar are ever found. There were probably not many made — the lid is certainly not very practical. When seen, they are found plain, banded, or mocha decorated. This example was made in East Liverpool, Ohio, where much yellow ware was produced. C. 1890. 7" tall. $850.00 – 950.00.

As I've said before, potters used the same molds for different types of clay. This pair of cookie jars is identical to some produced in blue and white stoneware. I like the form. They are big — 8" tall and 8½" at the widest part. Most likely Ohio, about 1910 to 1920. $150.00 – 225.00 each.

These are two of the three pieces I have seen like this. Although the form suggests that it is a saucepan for stovetop use, I think that it may be for oven use, like a pipkin. These pieces have a white lining and feet, like a nappy. I suspected that they were made by either Yellow Rock or Jeffords until finding a marked example confirmed this. (See section on Marks.) All three examples I've found have had their lids. I think that seeing three in 12 years qualifies them as rare! Length with handle, 9½" to 11". $350.00 – 450.00 each.

Like its Rockingham cousins, this piece is rare. It is the only example I have seen in plain yellow ware. Unfortunately, it does not have its lid, which would have been great for study purposes. The spout is bigger on this piece than on the Rockingham examples, otherwise it is very similar. I also attribute this to Jeffords. 11" across with handle. $350.00 – 450.00.

This Rockingham pipkin has a similar form to Bennington pipkins, with a straight handle instead of a curved one. A pipkin is another name for a bean pot for baking beans. They were made over a long time span but not many survived. I also attribute this piece to Jeffords — go back to the pair of Rockingham saucepans and look at the similarities. 8" in length including handle. $350.00 – 450.00.

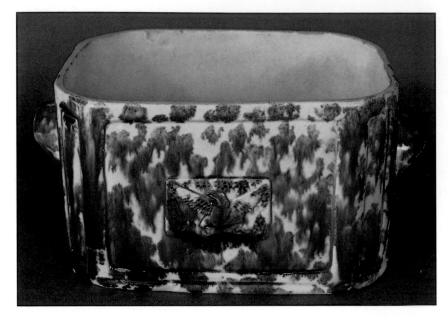

I've seen a few of these pieces but none of them ever had a lid. I'm very curious about what it may have looked like. This was probably just for storage and not for cooking. It is a rare form which is further elevated by the historical motif of an eagle with stars. I've been told that this may have been made in New Jersey, however, the way the Rockingham is applied reminds me of Otto Lewis — remember that tall coffee pot? About 9" long, 5½" tall. Mid-nineteenth century. $850.00 and up.

Two plain yellow storage jars, each with a small hole in the lid. I don't know if the holes are for aeration or possibly to insert a small knob for a finial. Although these are similar in size and shape to canning jars they aren't canning jars — they were never meant to be sealed. A hard-to-find form produced in Ohio, c. 1880. About 6" tall. $200.00 – 250.00 each.

This is a rare form for a bean pot in yellow ware. It has a lot of stone in the body, which is probably why it is in such good condition. The Rockingham looks like an afterthought. 6" tall. American, c. 1900. $350.00 – 450.00.

Beater jars are usually banded. It's unusual to find a sponged example. This one was made by the Morton Pottery in Illinois, about 1920 to 1930. $145.00 – 195.00.

There is no doubt about the intended purpose of this barrel-shaped jar with the lid finial being a pipe. 4½" tall. Possibly English or European, 1870 – 1900. $150.00 – 225.00.

This banded ovoid storage jar is very unusual. It would have had an inset lid that sat level with the bottom of the flared collar. Height is 7½". Definitely not American. 1850 – 1880. $300.00 – 400.00.

Yellow ware was made in many places, as evidenced by these large banded jars. They are marked MAASTRICHT and were made in Holland. Many collectors have trouble accepting yellow ware that was not made in the United States, as if that is the only "good" yellow ware. The clay is thin and the slip bands are very thick and dark. The pottery lids have been replaced by wooden ones. The height is 7½" and the jars date to around 1900. Each, $150.00 – 200.00.

Yellow ware covered serving dishes made in the nineteenth century are not often found. This is a beautiful example with its embossed grape motif. The applied handles and finial were well thought out — the piece is easy to grasp firmly. England, 1840 to 1870. 9½" long. $650.00 – 750.00.

Another Scottish piece in the typical colors, but an unusual form. The base has molded roses and the lid has a reclining dog for a finial. About 1870. Measures 5"x3¼". $450.00 – 550.00.

What a striking pitcher! The deep golden yellow body complements the bicolored earthworm. This piece is definitely American, possibly Pennsylvania or New York. Third quarter nineteenth century. 7½" tall. $1,750.00 and up.

I am sure that this tiny pitcher was part of a child's tea service. (Check the similarly decorated teapot in Tea & Coffee Pots.) The applied decoration is certainly something not seen on yellow ware. The detail is amazing. Early English pottery, pre-1850. 3¼" tall. $450.00 – 550.00.

Many miniature pitchers are part of a pitcher and bowl set — this one is not. The incising is something not normally found on pitchers of this size. It has a white lining. English, about third quarter nineteenth century. 2¾" tall. $400.00 – 475.00.

Left, a very unusual form for a miniature pitcher. Only 2¼" tall. Right, a nice form with great clay color. 3¾" tall. Both are most likely English, 1850 – 1900. Left, $400.00 – 475.00. Right, $350.00 – 450.00.

An interesting mocha design on this big, 10" tall pitcher. This design was the work of a skilled decorator — it shows great control and sensitivity. Some collectors would prefer darker seaweed but this pitcher makes up for in design what it lacks in stronger color. Check out the lift lug, embossed with the face of a lion! English or Scottish, c. 1870. $1,500.00 and up.

I like the ewer form of this mocha-decorated pitcher. Maybe at one time it had a matching bowl. It is rare to see this form in a large pitcher (7½" tall). The combination of brown seaweed and tricolored bands is unusual, too. The English refer to this as a pitcher because the body and spout are one. Pieces with applied spouts (which is nearly all of the pieces in this chapter) are referred to as jugs. English or Scottish, mid to late 1800s. $1,600.00 – 1,800.00.

This set of a pitcher and six mugs are referred to as Buckeye. They were made by the Morton Pottery Co. to be used as a giveaway (ah, the good, old days!) in a promotion for syrup. On the bottom they are impressed in script "Buckeye 100% Pure." This is a complete set. I discovered that when I was lucky enough to find an original box. It would be possible to assemble a set — the pitcher is the hardest piece to find. They were made around 1920. The set, $475.00 – 575.00. The pitcher alone, $100.00 – 150.00. Mugs, each, $50.00 – 60.00.

English yellow ware pitcher with dainty copper lustre decoration and a pink enamel rose. 6" tall. C. 1850. $175.00 – 225.00.

There are a lot of banded pitchers around but this one is exceptional. The slip bands that appear to be blue are actually white spattered with cobalt blue. The deep yellow clay is scroddled below the bands at the rim. Height is 8½". C. 1880. I attribute this pitcher to southeastern Pennsylvania, possibly Jeffords. $495.00 – 625.00.

Plain yellow yellow ware pitchers are not that easy to find. On the left, an embossed-band pitcher produced at Yellow Rock in Philadelphia, about 1870 to 1910. 5½" tall. Right, a beater jug, so-called because the inside is made like a beater jar. Brush-McCoy, about 1929. Also 5½" tall. Each, $150.00 – 200.00.

A rare pitcher, made by Wedgwood to celebrate the Centennial of the United States. Stars are embossed around the rim; states of the union are embossed on the ribbed band. Then, there is a brown transfer on each side — Independence Hall to represent 1776, Centennial Hall to represent 1876, both in Philadelphia. Finally, the dates 1776 and 1876 are embossed on the handle and outlined in brown slip. This pitcher is a history lesson in itself. 7⅜" tall. $750.00 – 850.00.

Two interesting mocha-decorated pitchers. Left, 10" tall with fist-sized blue seaweed flowers. England, last quarter nineteenth century. Right, the unusual form and atypically wide slip bands more than make up for the sparse blue seaweed. 8" tall. Possibly American, 1870 – 1890. Left, $1,500.00 – 1,700.00. Right, $1,250.00 – 1,400.00.

Three plain pitchers, all made in Ohio around 1915 to 1925. The pitcher on the left is from Brush-McCoy's Nurock line (only without the Rockingham); the others I cannot attribute to any particular pottery. The smallest pitcher has a lot of dark flecks in the clay (an indication of stone in the body) and a white lining. Height ranges from 5" to 7½". Each, $110.00 – 185.00.

This is not the typical Rockingham-decorated cow creamer. The light application of brown, along with the green on the base, makes it very unusual. It is the typical size and has Bennington-type characteristics. Expect damage to the horns, ears, tail, and missing lids. 1850 – 1860. $750.00 – 900.00.

This is one of the rarest, and best, mocha-decorated pitchers you will ever see. The decorator combed the slip bands after applying them. Multiple slip bands nicely complement the mocha band; the barrel-shaped form is unusual, too. About 8" tall. England, c. 1830. $3,500.00 and up.

I have shown these three pitchers to give you an idea of the yellow ware produced and used in Baltimore, MD. They were dug from a privy (that's right!) in that area. Privies were used as dumps — there was no trash collection then. Sometimes privy contents were the result of an accident, while emptying certain containers...you get my drift. Pieces like these are great for study purposes — I was thrilled to be able to have them. I am dating them 1850 to 1880.

Definitely an experiment! This is a pitcher from the Hull Pottery company — their blue-banded ware. This pitcher, however, was dipped in a pink lustre glaze after being slip-decorated. You can see the shape of the bands under the glaze. 5" tall. 1920 – 1930. $150.00 – 175.00.

Hound-handled pitchers are not easy to find. Ones like this Harker Taylor & Co. pitcher are seen less often than a New Jersey or Vermont example. The hound is distinctive because his posture is different from most hound handles. Check the section on Marks to see the mark that is on the bottom of this pitcher. East Liverpool, Ohio, 1846 – 1851. $1,500.00 and up.

There are a lot of interesting features packed into this 5" tall mocha pitcher. They are: the form, seen in early English pottery, c. 1840; the handle; the embossed spout; the white lining; and the background color for the seaweed, a blue/green/gray slip. The black seaweed is well defined and reminds me of tadpoles. One of my favorite pieces. $2,000.00 and up.

A pitcher with nice form and an extended spout, 9" tall. Varying shades of brown bands complement nicely the deep yellow clay. Ohio or Pennsylvania, 1865 – 1890. $375.00 – 450.00.

It is unusual to see yellow ware with blue sponged decoration. This 10" tall pitcher is Midwestern, c. 1910. $250.00 – 350.00.

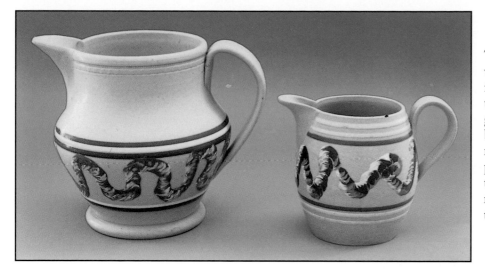

These are two *great* pieces of earthworm-decorated yellow ware! The form on both pieces is different and the quality of the decoration is very good. Also of interest: the rouletted band and the placement of the decoration on the pitcher on the left; the pearl ware glaze on the pitcher on the right. Height is 5½" and 3¾", respectively. Both are English, 1830 to 1850. Each, $1,850.00 and up.

This is generically called a toby pitcher, this one in particular, the snuff taker. They are not very common, especially in yellow ware with such a small amount of Rockingham. Regardless of the type of clay it is rare to find one of these pitchers with the original lid, which looks like the crown of the hat. 8" tall. England, c. 1840. $675.00 – 825.00.

A utilitarian pitcher with minimal bands. 6½" tall. Midwestern, about 1920. Pitchers like this one can be found in different sizes, and with blue and white bands instead of the black and white ones seen here. $145.00 – 185.00.

Super bicolored seaweed on this pitcher. The blue and green flowers are unusual — many of seaweed flowers are open at the top, like tulips. Remember, a pitcher that is bicolored on both sides, like this one, is more valuable than a similar pitcher with one color on each side. Possibly Ohio, 1870 to 1900. 7½" tall. $1,500.00 and up.

Yes, I know, this looks like a chamber pot, but take a look at that spout. This is another piece that was made as a gag for a pub. If the form didn't repel the drinker, the snuff taker and the reptiles inside would. Impressed around the rim is "PICK ME UP AND USE ME WELL AND WHAT I SEE I'LL NEVER TELL HAND IT OVER TO ME MY DEAR 1877." A unique piece at this time, although I'm sure some people will not appreciate the English sense of humor! The overall length is 13" — the overall height is 5½". $2,000.00 and up.

Pitchers

There are a number of these sanded-band pitchers around in all sizes and band combinations. This one is 3" tall. English, of course. $100.00 – 175.00.

The undulating seaweed on this pitcher is more like a band of earthworm than typical seaweed decoration. Perhaps the decorator was used to using earthworm. The coin-sized blip in the seaweed has a blue and white combination that resembles an arching dolphin. 8" tall. 1870 – 1890. $1,200.00 and up.

Although heavily embossed, this pitcher still has a primitive look to it. That funny little guy surrounded by nature — maybe it's supposed to be Adam in the Garden of Eden. I am not sure if this pitcher is American or English, but I do think it dates to about 1870. 7" tall. $375.00 – 475.00.

See the band combination at the top of this mocha pitcher? I think that it is indicative of pieces made by a pottery in Baltimore. The simple shape and thick, buff clay are other indicators, too. This pitcher was also dug from a privy in Baltimore. The flowing slip design is rare on yellow ware. 7" tall. 1840 – 1870. $2,000.00 and up.

The simple black seaweed design on this pitcher has bled into the white slip background, making it appear dark green. Also, it is unusual to see only white slip bands on a mocha-decorated piece. 9" tall. English, third quarter nineteenth century. $950.00 – 1,150.00.

Pale yellow slip is the rare background for this black seaweed mocha pitcher. The seaweed is bold on this otherwise delicate piece. England, 1850 to 1880. 4¼" tall. $750.00 – 875.00.

A variety of miniature pitchers. These had to be toys since they are too small to be practical. 3" to 4" tall. English, mid to late 1800s. $400.00 – 450.00 each.

I have seen identical seaweed designs on pearl ware mocha pitchers. Perhaps the decorator of this pitcher transferred his skill to yellow ware. It certainly is an unusual design. Sometimes this shape is referred to as baluster. This pitcher is American, c. 1870 I think. 7½" tall. $1,500.00 and up.

The decoration on this pitcher looks like an ocean wave (with droplets of water) and a flower. The spiral earthworm flower reminds me of a carnation. The blue and white bands are something special, too. This piece was obviously done by a skilled person. It is unusual to see a lift lug on an earthworm pitcher, but then, not many are this big. 9½" tall. England, c. 1850. $2,500.00 and up.

Plain yellow ware hound handle pitchers are rare. This one is a high quality example. The detail is so good that it was not hard to get a good photograph of it. The clay color is better than usual for a piece made by the American Pottery Co., New Jersey. C. 1840. 10" tall. $2,000.00 and up.

Although the seaweed on this pitcher is not in a scenic pattern, it is unusual nonetheless. Besides being bicolored, the seaweed is on two wide slip bands, instead of one. Definitely English, c. 1870 – 1900. 9½". $1,600.00 and up.

On the left is a rare pitcher made at Bennington. Yellow ware was frequently used as a body for majolica — this looks like a blank for that purpose. 5" tall. 1847 – 1858. The pitcher on the right is obviously a miniature but this time with blue seaweed decoration. Again, this form indicates that it was not part of a pitcher and bowl set. Note the tiny pulled spout instead of the applied spout seen on larger pitchers. Left, $350.00 – 450.00. Right, $850.00 – 950.00.

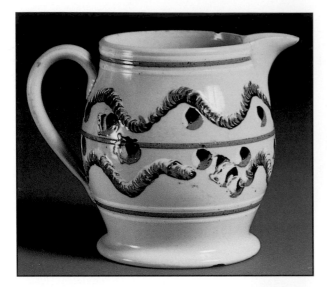

Very few pieces of yellow ware mocha are at this level. This pitcher is the ultimate in earthworm and cat's eye decoration, with a double row of undulating earthworm and many tricolored cat's eyes. It is English and 7½" tall. The date is c. 1850. $3,000.00 and up.

These are a fabulous pair. On the left is a jug which is rather plain until you get to that bold seaweed design. Obviously done by a very skilled decorator, the dots of seaweed form a diamond shape under an arch of short, horizontal blue seaweed stems. 8½" tall. On the right is a bicolored design in deep green and soft red. Again, a very strong allover design. 9½" tall. Both are English, 1850 – 1880. Left, $1,800.00 and up. Right, $2,500.00 and up.

Many bands on this small pitcher, only 3½" tall. American, c. 1900. $300.00 – 400.00.

Two plain pitchers with interesting details. Left, engine turned with a masked spout. Right, a fancy handle and allover embossing of vines and flowers. Both are English and about 4½" tall. 1850 – 1880. Each, $195.00 – 325.00.

One of the best seaweed pitchers ever. A fantastic bicolored design in blue and black seaweed and profuse slip bands. I think this piece speaks for itself. 9½" tall and English. It was made between 1850 and 1880. $2,500.00 and up.

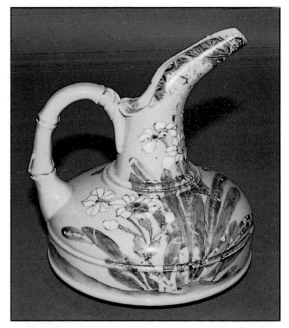

This pitcher was made for pouring oil, which makes sense when you see the spout. It has overglaze painting of flowers and leaves, and a bamboo-like handle with gilt trim. It is twentieth century, but I am sure it isn't American or English. There is an oval impressed mark on the bottom which cannot be deciphered. 4½" tall. $75.00 – 95.00.

This yellow ware pitcher has a lot of interesting details. The body has rouletted and engine-turned decoration, with pink lustre bands and a floral design under the spout. There are also applied decorations overlaid with pink lustre. On one side, a tree, and on the other side, a soldier with a drum and a firearm. English, c. 1850. 6" tall. $450.00 – 550.00.

I have saved the best for last in the Pitcher category. This is one of two pitchers known with this type of decoration. This pitcher was made to commemorate the laying of the cornerstone for the foundation of the Derbyshire (England) jail. The jail was located in Wooden Box, now known as Woodville, near Burton-on-Trent. It was given as a presentation piece to John Marshall, whose name is on the mocha band. He was a prominent merchant in the town. In script, "The Foundation for The 'Lock-up' at Wooden=Box Commenced October nineteenth, 1846." Besides being a piece with great historical significance, this pitcher has a rare and skillfully done mocha design in blue seaweed. England. 10" tall. $5,000.00 and up.

Glossary

Bennington: A generic term used to describe pottery made at the Bennington Pottery in Bennington, VT. The terms Bennington and Rockingham are not interchangeable. Rockingham is a glaze, Bennington is a place.

Cane ware: Yellow clay, mixed with stoneware, which is unglazed on the exterior, A dry, cane-colored appearance. From 1780 on.

Crazing: Cracking in the glaze due to exposure to heat and cold temperatures.

Embossed: A raised design, created by molding pottery in a mold.

Engine turning: Decorative geometric patterns cut into pottery by a lathe. The lathe would have been pre-set with a design that tended to cover a large area. From 1760 on.

Lustre: A metallic film coating the surface of a vessel. Either pink, silver, or copper.

Mocha: A broad (and often confusing) term used to describe a type of decoration (not clay body) used on creamware, pearl ware, yellow ware, ironstone, or redware. The decorations consist of slip (earthworm or cat's eye, for example) or seaweed, which was a liquid (oxides, nicotine, stale urine) poured on wet slip; this liquid bled into the wet slip causing dendritic (moss-like) designs.

Pearl ware: A white earthenware body with a glaze containing cobalt (blue); also used to describe a glaze.

Polychrome: Two or more colors.

Rockingham: A purple-brown glaze created at the Rockingham pottery, Swinton, England, in the late 1700s.

Rouletting: Decorative geometric patterns cut into pottery with a brass tool similar to a pie crimper. Usually a single band and near the rim or shoulder of a vessel.

Scroddled: Giving a marbled or swirled effect, can be used to describe clay *or* slip decoration.

Slip: Liquified clay, used mostly for surface decoration.

Stoneware: A hard, high fired clay.

Transfer printing: A scene on tissue paper, dipped in ink and then wrapped around or laid over a piece of pottery, hence the name transfer ware.

Yellow ware: Earthenware, sometimes combined with stoneware, defined by its color, regardless of color intensity.

Barrett, Richard Carter. *Bennington Pottery and Porcelain: A Guide To Identification*. New York: Crown Publishers, Inc., 1958.

Branin, Lelyn M. *The Early Makers of Handcrafted Earthenware and Stoneware in Central and Southern New Jersey*. New Jersey: Associated University Presses, Inc., 1988.

Creswick, Alice M. *Red Book No. 6: The Collector's Guide To Old Fruit Jars*. Grand Rapids, MI: Alice M. Creswick, 1990.

Denker, Ellen and Bert. *The Warner Collector's Guide to North American Pottery and Porcelain*. New York: Warner Books, Inc., 1982.

Denker, Ellen and Paul. *The Kirkpatrick's Pottery at Anna, Illinois*. Crouse Printing and Mailing, 1986.

Gallo, John. *Nineteenth and Twentieth Century Yellow Ware*. New York: Heritage Press, 1985.

Godden, Geoffrey A. *Encyclopedia of British Pottery and Porcelain Marks*. New York: F.R.S.A. Bonanza Books, MCMLXIV.

Hall, Doris and Burdell. *Morton's Potteries: 99 Years*. Nixa, MO: A and J Printers, 1982.

Lechler, Doris Anderson. *English Toy China*. Marietta, OH: Antique Publications, 1989.

Lehner, Lois. *Lehner's Encyclopedia of U.S. Marks on Pottery, Porcelain, and Clay*. Paducah, KY: Collector Books, 1988.

Lewis, John and Griselda. *Prattware English and Scottish Relief Decorated and Underglaze Colored Earthenware 1780 – 1840*. Antique Collector's Club, 1984.

Leibowitz, Joan. *Yellow Ware: The Transitional Ceramic*. Exton, PA: Schiffer Publishing, 1985.

McAllister, Lisa S. and Michel, John L. *Collecting Yellow Ware*. Paducah, KY: Collector Books, 1993.

McNerney, Kathryn. *Blue and White Stoneware: An Identification and Value Guide*. Paducah, KY: Collector Books, 1981.

Miller, J. Jefferson, II. *English Yellow-Glazed Earthenware*. Washington D.C.: Smithsonian Institution Press, 1974.

Rickard, Jonathan. *How To Speak English Ceramics*. Maine Antique Digest. April, 1992.

Rinker, Harry L. *Warman's Antiques and Their Prices*. Wallace-Homestead Book Company, 1990.

Roberts, Brenda. *The Collector's Encyclopedia of Hull Pottery*. Paducah, KY: Collector Books, 1980.

Sanford, Martha and Steve. *The Guide to Brush-McCoy Pottery*. Clarksville, TN: Jostens, Inc., 1992.

Towner, Donald. *Creamware*. Faber and Faber, 1984.

Webster, D.B. *The Brantford Pottery 1849–1907*. Ontario: University of Toronto Press, 1968.

Wetherbee, Jean. *A Second Look at White Ironstone*. Wallace-Homestead Book Company, 1985.

Wilson, Hewitt. *Ceramics Clay Technology*. New York, NY: McGraw-Hill Book Company, Inc., 1927.

Schroeder's
ANTIQUES
Price Guide

. . . is the #1 best-selling antiques & collectibles value guide on the market today, and here's why . . .

• *More than 300 advisors, well-known dealers, and top-notch collectors work together with our editors to bring you accurate information regarding pricing and identification.*

• *More than 45,000 items in almost 500 categories are listed along with hundreds of sharp original photos that illustrate not only the rare and unusual, but the common, popular collectibles as well.*

• *Each large close-up shot shows important details clearly. Every subject is represented with histories and background information, a feature not found in any of our competitors' publications.*

• *Our editors keep abreast of newly developing trends, often adding several new categories a year as the need arises.*

If it merits the interest of today's collector, you'll find it in *Schroeder's*. And you can feel confident that the information we publish is up to date and accurate. Our advisors thoroughly check each category to spot inconsistencies, listings that may not be entirely reflective of market dealings, and lines too vague to be of merit. Only the best of the lot remains for publication.

Without doubt, you'll find
SCHROEDER'S ANTIQUES PRICE GUIDE
the only one to buy for
reliable information and values.

cb

COLLECTOR BOOKS
A Division of Schroeder Publishing Co., Inc.